The Dishonorable Dr. Cook

THE DISHONORABLE DR. COOK

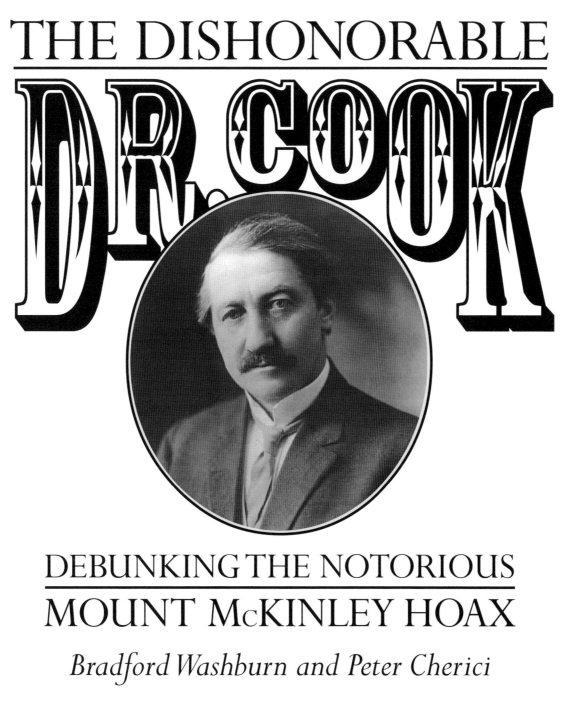

DEBUNKING THE NOTORIOUS
MOUNT McKINLEY HOAX

Bradford Washburn and Peter Cherici

THE MOUNTAINEERS BOOKS

Published by
The Mountaineers Books
1001 SW Klickitat Way, Suite 201
Seattle, WA 98134

Published simultaneously in Great Britain by Cordee, 3a DeMontfort Street, Leicester, England, LE1 7HD

Manufactured in Canada

Editor: Kathleen Cubley
Copy Editor: Cynthia Newman Bohn
Cover, book design, and layout: Ani Rucki
Mapmakers: Dee Molenaar and Ani Rucki

All photographs by Bradford Washburn unless otherwise noted. When available, Washburn negative numbers are listed with captions.

We gratefully acknowledge all those who provided photographs for this book. We have made every effort to trace and contact copyright holders and gain permission for such use. If an error or omission is brought to our notice we will be pleased to remedy the situation in future editions of this book. For further information, please contact the publisher.

Cover photograph: *Dr. Frederick A. Cook* (Courtesy Byrd Polar Research Center Archival Program)

Pages 14/15, 98/99, 105, and 108: *Mount McKinley, Alaska*. Map by Bradford Washburn © 1990 Swiss Foundation for Alpine Research, Zurich, Switzerland and University of Alaska Press, Fairbanks, Alaska

Library of Congress Cataloging-in-Publication Data
Washburn, Bradford, 1910–
    The dishonorable Dr. Cook : debunking the notorious McKinley hoax / by Bradford Washburn and Peter Cherici.— 1st ed.
      p. cm.
    Includes bibliographical references (p.).
    ISBN 0-89886-804-1 (hard cover)
    1. McKinley, Mount (Alaska)—Discovery and exploration. 2. Cook, Frederick Albert, 1865–1940. 3. Explorers—Alaska—McKinley, Mount—Biography. 4. Mountaineers—Alaska—McKinley, Mount—Biography. 5. Impostors and imposture—Alaska—McKinley, Mount—History—20th century. I. Title: Dishonorable Doctor Cook. II. Cherici, Peter, 1948– III. Title.
F912.M2 W34 2001
917.98'3—dc21   2001003190

To Ed Barrill,

Belmore Browne,

Herschel Parker,

and Bob Dunn.

They knew the truth from the very beginning.

—B.W.

The test of an explorer's work must always be in context of the quality of his work. His published narrative, with its complete data, is his book of rights. Peary's book and mine were printed twenty years ago. Nothing can be added, nothing subtracted. The material thus presented, reexamined and compared with later work of later explorers, verifies or condemns. History thus gives to each explorer his award of merit. It can be done in no other way. Public opinion, news reports, encyclopedic information, may influence the casual observer—but writers of history get their information from original sources. I reached the Pole. I climbed McKinley. The controversy, from my angle, is at an end. I now have other still more important exploration at hand. This will occupy my attention until the frost of the next world arrives.

—Dr. Frederick A. Cook
From an unpublished autobiography stored in the Library of Congress,
as quoted in *Hero in Disgrace*, by Howard S. Abramson

Contents

PART II

EXPOSED BY FACT AND PHOTO

PREFACE

In March and April 1953, Dick Kleber, David Fisher, and I spent a month surveying the southeastern approaches of Mount McKinley. This was the last of the unmapped wilderness that surrounded the great peak before the publication of our Mount McKinley map, which was published in 1960.

Assuming we'd have to ride out several big storms before our work was finished, I brought with me a copy of Dr. Frederick A. Cook's *To the Top of the Continent,* as where we were to do our work was the epicenter of the area where Cook and Ed Barrill were supposed to have made their climb ninety-seven years ago.

Don Sheldon—the famous bush pilot who was in charge of flying us with our supplies from Talkeetna to our base camp—and I thought that it would be good fun to do a little detective work together. After all, a few minutes in Don's tiny Super Cub airplane would easily cover an hour's walk on snowshoes in that completely glaciated wilderness.

With Cook's book in my lap, we set out to see if we could locate Dr. Cook's Fake Peak, which we knew must be at almost exactly the same altitude as our 5,000-foot camp. After reading Belmore Browne's book *The Conquest of Mount McKinley,* which told us exactly where to look, we were circling around it in less than ten minutes. Then, as we circled very low over this area, to our astonishment we actually discovered what seemed to be the location at which Dr. Cook had taken his famous photograph titled "The Silent Glory and Snowy Wonder of the Upper World, 15,400 feet" though our altimeter was showing an altitude of only 5,000 feet.

A few yards away, we found a beautiful landing spot and without even needing snowshoes, we hiked a hundred yards to the little pass from which that picture must have been taken. With Dr. Cook's book in hand, we turned to page 226 and there we were exactly. And less than a mile south of us, squarely in the middle of that picture, stood Dr. Cook's famous Fake Peak.

There wasn't a bit of snow where we stood in the windswept little pass, and squarely at our feet was a tiny one-pint fuel can—and as we scuffed in the gravel, a yard or two from the can was a small cloth food bag. Dr. Cook and Ed Barrill must have had lunch there—right where we stood!

In all, Dr. Cook had taken fewer than a dozen pictures, and here in a half-hour, we'd precisely located two of them. As we flew back to our camp, I realized that we'd resolved at least a quarter of the Cook mystery in less than a single morning. It's taken nearly half a century to resolve the rest of the details. This book does exactly that.

Bradford Washburn

June 21, 2001

INTRODUCTION

In the early years of the twentieth century, the exploration of the Earth's polar regions and the Far North gripped the imagination of the general public much as the exploration of space would fascinate them some six decades later. The Arctic and Antarctic were almost untouched and there were vast areas of Greenland where no one had ever set foot, while parts of Alaska and northern Canada had been visited only by the native peoples of those regions. Becoming the first Westerner to set eyes on these strange and distant lands became an obsession for explorers and adventurers, many of them lured by the prospect of enduring fame.

A successful explorer's fame would be well warranted. The obstacles to be overcome were formidable: extreme cold, totally unknown and rugged terrain, the possibility of starvation if food and water supplies ran out, the danger of unexpected mishaps, and finally the complex logistics of outfitting an expedition. The last task was in some ways the most daunting. Mounting an expedition was an enormously expensive undertaking. Explorers and climbers had to be outfitted with the best possible equipment—to do less would endanger lives. Transportation had to be arranged both en route and at the destination. Food and fuel for the journey had to be secured and paid for—no small effort for a group that included packers and pack animals in addition to various assistants ranging from medical personnel to photographers. And salaries had to be paid.

For explorers the quest for funding was almost as difficult as the journey itself. Government support was nonexistent, and while several local and national geographic and natural history societies did exist, the amounts they could contribute were usually nominal. Wealthy sportsmen or philanthropists with an interest in exploration occasionally provided financial backing, but their support usually came at the price of including them or one of their relatives as part of the expedition. Another method of raising money was to award a newspaper or magazine the exclusive rights to an explorer's story in return for payment in advance—an approach that became increasingly popular as the public's appetite for vicariously experiencing heroic adventures continued to grow.

Explorers and their feats were thus much in the public mind when in late September of 1906, Dr. Frederick A. Cook walked out of the Alaskan wilderness and announced that he had just become the first person to climb Mount McKinley, which at close to 20,000 feet was by far the highest peak in North America. Since up to this time few peaks in the Alaskan Far North had been explored, his announcement was greeted with great excitement.

News of this remarkable achievement spread rapidly, and Cook was soon being lionized as a national hero. Depicted in the press as a gentleman adventurer, an intrepid explorer who embodied the American ideal, he was invited to lecture at the prestigious American Alpine Club in New York and feted at numerous dinners held in his honor. Initially only a tiny few questioned Cook's claim. He had already made somewhat of a name for himself as an explorer, having participated in expeditions to Greenland with Robert E. Peary and to Antarctica with Roald Amundson, and he was one of the founders of both the American Alpine Club and the Explorers Club. Furthermore, explorers in those days generally belonged to an educated and aristocratically minded elite who believed a gentleman's word to be tantamount to a sacred pledge. In this rarified world it was unthinkable that anyone would violate this unspoken code.

But as the details of Cook's climb became public, controversy began to brew. There was something not quite right about Cook's story, and when challenged on various points, the great hero was vague and inconsistent. A few experienced mountaineers, concerned with protecting the integrity of their profession, began to dig for the truth. Thus begins one of the twentieth century's great detective stories. Had Dr. Cook make it to top of Mount McKinley or hadn't he?

Part I

THE EXTRAORDINARY DR. COOK

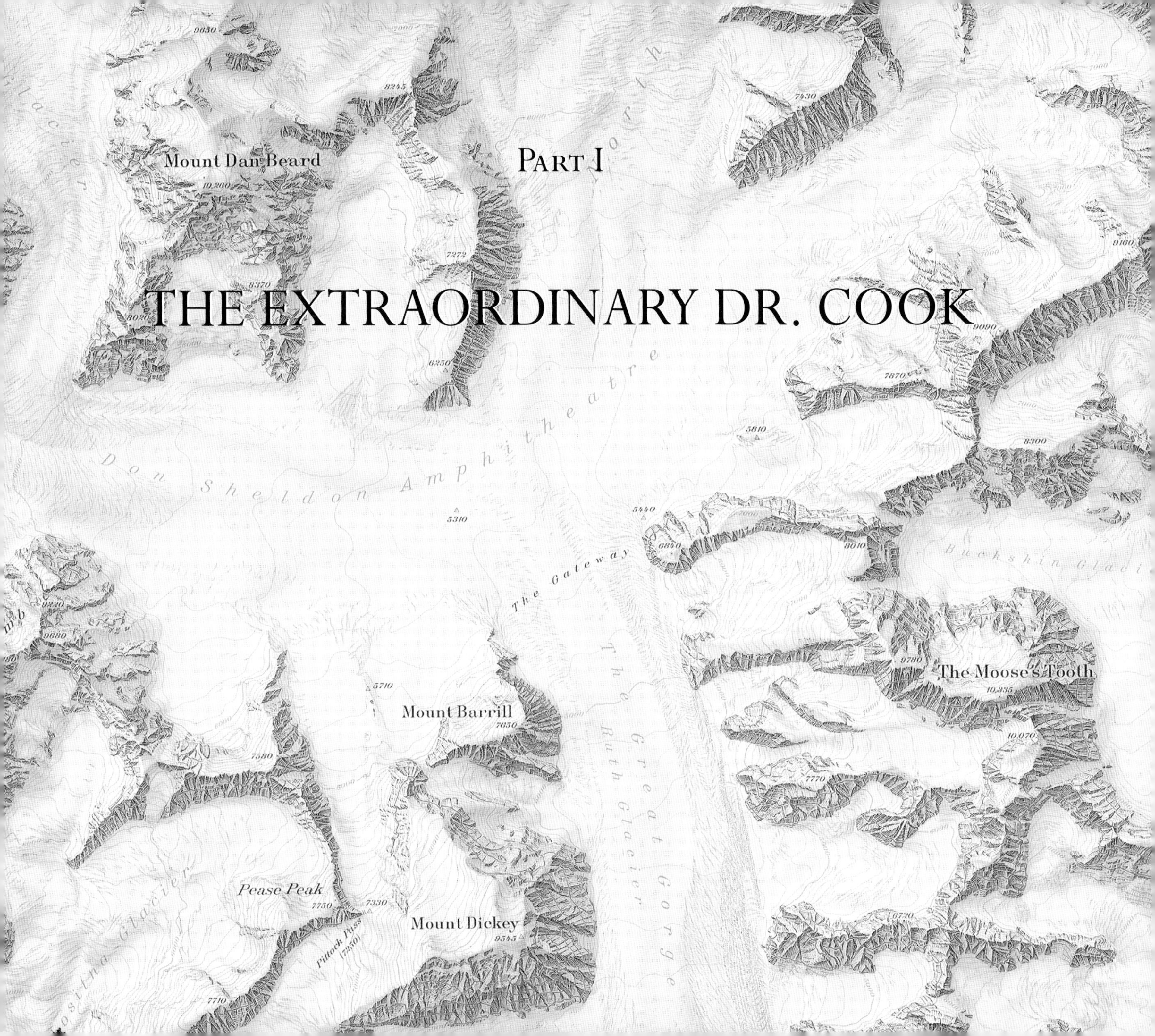

Mount Dan Beard
10,260
8245
7430
7272
8370
6250
9160
9090
7870
5810
8300
Don Sheldon Amphitheatre
5310
5440
6840
8010
The Gateway
The Great Gorge
Ruth Glacier
5710
Mount Barrill
7650
7580
9780
The Moose's Tooth
10,335
10,070
7770
Pease Peak
7750
7330
Pittock Pass
(7250)
Mount Dickey
9545
6720
7710

BIBLIOGRAPHIC ENTRY AND ACKNOWLEDGMENT

The Mountaineers Books and the authors would like to gratefully acknowledge the valuable work of Robert M. Bryce in *Cook & Peary: The Polar Controversy Resolved,* Stackpole Books, Mechanicsburg, Pa. (1997; 1,133 pages). The work covers the life of Dr. Frederick A. Cook and is illustrated with photos, maps, and sketches, and fully annotated with over 2,000 footnotes. The authors relied on this seminal reference for important factual information not previously published about Dr. Cook's early life and his subsequent claims to have climbed Mount McKinley. We regret the omission of proper credit and citation in the original bibliography for *The Dishonorable Dr. Cook.*

CHAPTER 1

The Great Ice Mountain

Mount McKinley is not only the highest peak in North America, it is also the defining feature of Alaska's terrain. Located in the heart of the Alaska Range, McKinley looms far above the smaller peaks surrounding it and on clear days is visible as far south as Anchorage and as far north as Fairbanks. Snow cloaks its summit year-round and lengthy glaciers flow down its barren, windswept slopes. According to the traditions of the Susitna and other native peoples who dwell in its shadows, spirits both good and evil haunt the mountain's crags and icy crevasses.

Captain George Vancouver first sighted Mount McKinley on May 6, 1794, during his stubborn effort to find the Northwest Passage. Anchored in an arm of the ocean opposite the site of modern-day Anchorage—and more than 140 miles south of the giant peaks of the Alaska Range—he saw "distant stupendous mountains covered with snow, and apparently detached from one another." This is generally accepted as the first recorded mention of McKinley and its lofty partner, Mount Foraker. Because Vancouver did not venture inland, he had no appreciation of the peak's vast size, and its remoteness kept it shrouded in mystery for more than a hundred years.

In the 1830s Baron Ferdinand von Wrangell drew a rough map showing the location of Mount McKinley. An admiral in the Russian navy, Wrangell was famous for his explorations of the Siberian Arctic. After Czar Nicholas I appointed him governor of Alaska—which at the time was part of the Russian Empire—Wrangell sponsored the first serious exploration of the interior. He dispatched employees of the Russian American Company, which had a monopoly on the Alaska fur trade, to gather information on topography and native tribes. One of Wrangell's explorers was André Glazunov, the son of a Russian father and Aleut mother who had been reared in Alaska. Glazunov journeyed up the

Kuskokwim River until he was fifty miles west of "a great mountain called Tenada," the name bestowed on it by an interior tribe. From the information Glazunov and other Russian explorers brought back, Wrangell drew the first map of the Alaskan interior.

After the United States purchased Alaska in 1867, American explorers took up the task of scouting the interior. In the late 1870s, a prospector named Arthur Harper traveled along the Tanana River, which flows on the north side of the Alaska Range. From a point near the location of modern-day Fairbanks, he reported seeing "a great ice mountain to the south." The next American explorer to describe the mountain was Frank Densmore. In 1889 he came close to its base when he led an expedition along the north side of the Alaska Range, journeying from the Tanana to the Kuskokwim River. It was called Densmores Mountain for quite some time, but the general public never accepted this name with much enthusiasm.

It was not until 1897 that McKinley received its current name from William Dickey, a Princeton graduate with a talent for mathematics. After several failed business ventures in Seattle, Dickey tried his hand at Alaskan prospecting—and wrote dispatches to the *New York Sun* about his adventures. After journeying inland, he began prospecting with several others on the gravel bars near the end of the Ruth Glacier. He carried with him an instrument to measure angles and developed a surveying system that roughly positioned McKinley's summit. It quickly became apparent to him that the big peak was extremely high. To the astonishment of Dickey and his companions, his calculations yielded an altitude of approximately 20,000 feet.

At the end of the summer, Dickey and his friends had found no gold and had rafted down the Susitna River on their way back to civilization. As they drifted by Susitna Station they saw a man at the big dock and yelled to him for news about the "outside." He responded that William McKinley was the Republican candidate for the presidency. McKinley was a supporter of the gold standard, which would tie the price of silver to that of gold. This news dismayed Dickey's companions. They were ardent populists who had harangued Dickey daily on the benefits of "free silver." To spite his companions, Dickey named the mountain after McKinley, even though he had not yet been elected. In a letter of January 24, 1897, to the *New York Sun,* he proposed McKinley as the name for the mountain, and both the public and mapmakers quickly adopted his suggestion.

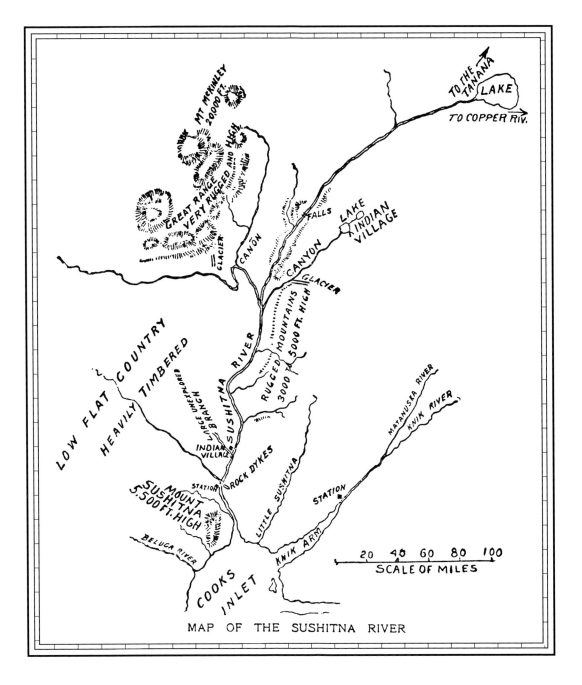

MT. MCKINLEY 20,000 FT.

GREAT RANGE VERY RUGGED AND HIGH

GLACIER

CAÑON

TO THE TANANA

LAKE

TO COPPER RIV.

FALLS

LAKE

INDIAN VILLAGE

CAÑON

GLACIER

LOW FLAT COUNTRY

HEAVILY TIMBERED

RUGGED MOUNTAINS 5000 FT. HIGH 3000 FT.

LARGE UNEXPLORED BRANCH

SUSHITNA RIVER

MATANUSKA RIVER

KNIK RIVER

INDIAN VILLAGE

ROCK DYKES

STATION

LITTLE SUSHITNA

STATION

MOUNT SUSHITNA 5,500 FT. HIGH

BELUGA RIVER

KNIK ARM

20 40 60 80 100
SCALE OF MILES

COOKS INLET

MAP OF THE SUSHITNA RIVER

The first time the name Mount McKinley appears on a map is in this 1897 rendering of the area by prospector William Dickey.

Dickey's report that Mount McKinley appeared to be the highest peak in North America excited the imagination of mountaineers and cartographers. The public's attention, however, was quickly diverted by the 1898 gold rush in the Klondike, with its romantic mystique of hardy prospectors braving the wilderness in search of riches. Consequently, little mention was made in newspapers of the U.S. Geological Survey expedition of George Eldridge and Robert Muldrow in 1899 to determine the true height of the mountain. Having run a surveyor's line up the Susitna River, Eldridge and Muldrow made observations on McKinley's summit from six different locations and computed its height to be 20,464 feet, which is remarkably close to its actual height of 20,320 feet—and only slightly higher than Dickey's rough estimate. They also plotted the mountain's position at latitude 63° 05' north and longitude 151° 00' west. Afterward, the achievement of these two professional surveyors was commemorated when two of the mountain's largest glaciers were named after them.

The same summer that Eldridge and Muldrow were studying Mount McKinley, a second U.S. Geological Survey party led by Josiah Spurr succeeded in making the first crossing of the Alaska Range. They boated and trekked up the Yentna and Skwentna Rivers, then made their way through Simpsons Pass. They reached the Kuskokwim River, headed toward Bristol Bay, then recrossed the Alaska Range via Katmai Pass to reach Cook Inlet. Their objective was to find a practical route for a road and railroad to connect Cook Inlet with Fairbanks. At the time, Anchorage had not yet been founded and the main settlement on the inlet was the small town of Tyonek. Although Spurr failed to find a suitable route for a road through the mountains, he did contribute greatly to knowledge of the vast wilderness southwest of Mount McKinley.

In 1902 Alfred H. Brooks of the U.S. Geological Survey was the first person to actually set foot on the mountain's slopes. His lengthy exploration of the northwest side of the Alaska Range that summer is still considered the most exhaustive and professional of all the early explorations of interior Alaska. In early August he camped on the banks of Slippery Creek, sixteen miles north of McKinley's summit. Leaving the rest of his party in camp, he hiked up onto a spur of the mountain as far as the snow line at 6,300 feet, nine miles from the summit. His objective was not to try for the summit but to closely examine the geological structure of the great peak. To mark his presence on McKinley's slopes, he buried a rifle cartridge and a note under a rock cairn, which, amazingly, was discovered by another U.S. Geological Survey party in 1954.

To confirm his predecessors' preliminary estimates of Mount McKinley's height, Brooks also performed a survey, observing a series of angles aimed at the summit from several new locations to the west, north, and northeast of the peak. His results indicated that the mountain was indeed more than 20,000 feet in height. In addition to making a rough map of the terrain, he recorded the various names used by the Alaskan tribes for the mountain. Among those who lived in the interior, it was known as Denali, a name that is frequently used today by both climbers and environmentalists. The natives living south of the Alaska Range knew it as Traleika, and the Russians who explored the western approaches to the range called it Bolshaia Gora. In essence, all of these names mean "The Great One." Brooks also published an article in the January 1903 issue of *National Geographic Magazine* suggesting that the best way to climb the mountain was from the north. After his survey, he was convinced that any other direction of approach would be too complex as well as dangerous.

With the data collected by Eldridge, Muldrow, and Brooks, not only did explorers and mountaineers begin to appreciate the uniqueness of Mount McKinley, but so did the public. The other great mountains of the world rise from lofty plateaus, as in Tibet, but McKinley's 20,000 feet rose directly out of a forested lowland that lay less than a thousand feet above the sea. There is also no mountain anywhere in the world even close to McKinley's height at such a high latitude as 63° north. McKinley's summit lies more than 2,400 miles farther north than Mount Everest. Furthermore, McKinley is located deep in Alaska's interior. To climb it mountaineers would have to haul all the food, fuel, and gear they would need across hundreds of miles of rugged, unexplored terrain before they could even begin an ascent. A summer climbing expedition would have to rely on horses to carry supplies, but grass for grazing grew for only a few months, limiting the time available to approach and climb the great peak. A winter expedition would have to travel by dogsled and contend with frigid temperatures and high winds, as well as having only a few hours of daylight. Thus, the great ice mountain duplicates polar conditions and the first person to reach its summit was certain to win acclaim almost as great as that which the public was reserving for the first person to reach the North or South Pole.

CHAPTER 2

Frederick Albert Cook, Adventurer

Frederick Albert Cook was born on June 10, 1865, to Theodore and Magdalena (née Long) Koch in the small town of Hortonville, New York, about seventy miles northwest of Manhattan. His father was a German immigrant and physician who had served as a medical officer with the Union Army during the Civil War. Frustrated by the various attempts of his comrades to pronounce his surname, Theodore Koch anglicized it to Cook. When Frederick was five, his father died of pneumonia, leaving the family impoverished. Magdalena used the money from a small life insurance policy to build a house and tried to eke out a living at odd jobs.

Even as a boy, Cook liked to have adventures and visit forbidden places—including a swimming hole where he almost drowned. In an autobiographical article written in 1911, he recalled leaping into the water even knowing that he could not swim. "Though I nearly gave out, in that short time I learned to swim. It seems to me now I have been swimming and struggling ever since." His self-reliance was evident early. His older brother, Will, would recall that young Fred rarely asked for help, believing he could accomplish even the most difficult tasks single-handedly. This boyish bravado would mature into a brash belief that he could overcome any obstacle.

By 1878 Magdalena Cook could no longer afford to stay in rural New York. She rented out the house in Hortonville and moved the family to Port Jervis, New York. To supplement the family's income, twelve-year-old Frederick held part-time jobs in a glass factory and as a lamplighter while attending school. A year later Magdalena moved the family again, this time to the Williamsburg section of Brooklyn after another of Frederick's older brothers, Theodore, found steady employment in a beer keg factory.

At age sixteen, Cook graduated from grammar school in Brooklyn, but poverty kept him from immediately going on to high school. He started a moderately-successful business printing calling cards and advertising circulars—or "broadsides" as they were called in those days. He attended high school at night, and after he graduated, Magdalena encouraged him to follow his father into the medical profession. At the time, the only prerequisites for admission to medical school were for a candidate to be of good moral character and at least twenty-one years old. In order to raise enough money for tuition, Cook sold his printing business and used the proceeds to start a milk delivery route with Theodore. Because they were supplying a new, creamier milk that had not been available in Brooklyn, the Cook Brothers Milk and Cream Company prospered. By 1887 Cook had saved enough money to attend Columbia University's College of Physicians and Surgeons, paying a reduced fee as the son of a physician. Nonetheless, he had to continue working with his brother in the milk business to meet his living expenses.

In medical school, Cook followed a grueling schedule with dogged determination. He worked from 1:00 A.M. to 7:00 A.M. delivering milk. Then he was faced with an hour and a half commute to 23rd Street in Manhattan, where Columbia's classes were then held. He attended class until 4:00 P.M. then returned to Brooklyn to sleep and study in the time remaining before he had to again report to work. Less than a year after he began medical school, Columbia moved its facilities to 59th Street. Since this would mean an extra hour of commuting that Cook could not accomplish with his already tight schedule, he transferred to New York University, which held classes near Washington Square.

Despite having little time for leisure, Cook met and courted Libby Forbes, marrying her in 1889. She was expecting their first child about the same time that Cook sat for his final examinations in 1890. When Libby went into labor, Cook called in a homeopathic physician to attend the delivery. Complications followed and Cook's daughter was born dead. A week later, peritonitis claimed Libby's life.

Shortly afterward, Cook learned that he had passed his medical examinations. The news did little to relieve his depression at losing his wife and child. He sold his share of the milk business to Theodore and tried to cultivate a medical practice on West 55th Street in Manhattan, but patients were slow to seek his services. To fill his time, he began to read about polar explorations, particularly the adventures of Dr. Elisha Kent Kane, a physician who had led a major expedition to the Arctic in the mid-1800s. Then in the spring of 1891, Cook chanced on a notice in the *New York Telegram* indicating that Lieutenant Robert E. Peary was about to set off on an expedition to determine how far north the land mass of Greenland extended. Cook immediately sent a telegram to Peary, offering his services as physician to the expedition.

Several weeks later, Peary responded by inviting Cook to his home in Philadelphia for an interview. When Cook arrived, Peary greeted him wearing his full-dress Navy uniform and outlined his plan to stay in northern Greenland during the winter of 1892–93, then explore northward in the spring. After they discussed Cook's qualifications as a physician and his ability to withstand the hardships of the Arctic, Peary offered him a place on his Wintering Expedition. In Cook's unpublished memoirs, he mentions that he thought Peary was "a thoroughly decent fellow, and a strong character." This first impression would change dramatically when Cook began to regard himself as Peary's rival.

A PASSION FOR THE ARCTIC

During Cook's first visit to the Far North, he was one of seven people who spent the winter in northern Greenland with Peary. In addition to his medical duties, Cook was appointed the expedition's ethnologist, charged with learning as much as he could about the native way of life. Discovering how the native population dealt with the problems of travel, hunting, clothing, and fuel was essential if the members of the expedition were to venture far inland. In later years, Cook wrote with his typical flair for the dramatic "no explorer can do much in the polar regions without this native insight to deliver life safely through the dangerous periods of famine and frost ever on the horizon of this world in white."

The first opportunity Cook had to distinguish himself came when the ship in which they were sailing to Greenland struck a small iceberg, causing an iron tiller to hit Peary's leg, breaking his ankle in two places. Although another physician who was on board set the break, Cook took charge of caring for Peary. For a number of days, Peary was in great pain and confined to his bunk. Cook administered morphine and constructed a splint-box to prevent the leg from banging against the bunk's side in rough weather. Several of the expedition's scientists suggested that they turn back. However, Cook assured them that Peary would recover with time and rest—which indeed he did—and the expedition continued on.

Peary's team landed at Inglefield Gulf on the northwest coast of Greenland. They built a wooden structure designed to endure the rigors of an arctic winter, which they called Redcliffe House after the red sandstone cliffs behind it. As the long arctic night set in, Cook began to gather anthropological data on the Eskimos living nearby. He visited an Eskimo camp, trading food and goods for native artifacts which Peary hoped to display in an exhibit at the World's Columbian Exposition, slated to open in Chicago in the summer of 1893. He also convinced several families to move closer to Redcliffe House, so he could study them throughout the winter. He took the Eskimos' body measurements, recorded their customs, and learned the rudiments of their language. The information he brought back to the United States won him widespread praise in the scientific community and a nomination as a member of the American Ethnological Association.

By the time spring came, Peary's ankle had fully healed. He set out northward across Greenland's central ice cap with Cook, Evind Astrup, and Langdon Gibson. On the early part of this journey, a disaster struck that demonstrates how little experience this group had with arctic conditions. When halting for the night on the ice cap, they made an amateurish shelter by covering a hollow with skis, then placing blocks of hard snow atop the skis. They fell asleep inside this makeshift ice hut, leaving their clothes outside of their sleeping bags. During the night a gale sprang up which quickly eroded the blocks, burying their clothes and exposing them to the wind. Forced to stay inside their sleeping bags for warmth, they were unable to move about to repair the damage. The storm lasted for several days. When it let up, Peary managed to dig his clothes from beneath the snow and then helped the others. After they had traveled 130 miles it became necessary to conserve supplies, so Cook and Gibson returned to Redcliffe House. Peary and Astrup continued north until they reached Independence Bay on the northeast side of Greenland, then returned to Redcliffe House by traveling along the coast. Although Cook had been a part of the first trek across Greenland, the majority of the fame and glory fell to Peary as leader of the expedition.

Perhaps Cook had joined Peary's expedition mainly to escape his grief, but after his experience in Greenland, polar exploration became his passion. When Peary asked him to accompany another party departing for northern Greenland in 1894, he eagerly accepted. To help raise funds and generate publicity for the new expedition, Cook gave a series of lectures based on his observations of the Eskimo, the proceeds of which he had to share with Peary. His talks were so successful that Herbert Bridgman, publisher of the *Brooklyn Standard Union,* proposed that Cook write a series of stories for the newspaper. This posed a difficulty. Peary had required all members of his 1892–93 expedition to sign contracts agreeing not to publish anything about their Greenland experience until one year after Peary's own account was published. Cook asked Peary to make an exception, but Peary refused. Cook then resigned as a member of Peary's upcoming expedition. The two did not publicly quarrel over this issue, but the incident appears to mark the beginning of Cook's unspoken rivalry with Peary.

Dr. Cook now opened a medical office in Brooklyn, which, due to his newfound fame as a member of Peary's expedition, fared better than his earlier practice. He continued lecturing on Eskimo culture, receiving generous stipends for appearances, which he no longer had to share with Peary. After a talk at Yale University, Cook was approached by Professor James Hoppin who proposed providing $10,000 to finance a small expedition to Greenland if Hoppin's son, Benjamin, was included in the party. Cook eagerly agreed to the plan, which would give him exactly what he coveted—a position as the leader of his own polar expedition.

On July 10, 1894, the sloop *Zeta* sailed from Halifax for the west coast of Greenland. Aboard were Cook, his assistant, E. H. Sutherland, Benjamin Hoppin, and sportsman Robert Perry, who had paid Cook $1,000 for the opportunity to hunt arctic game. When the vessel stopped at the small coastal settlements, Cook did not venture far inland, and as a result the expedition added nothing to the knowledge of Greenland's geography. He scored a publicity coup, however, by bringing several Eskimo children and sled dogs back to New York, where their adventures were widely followed by the newspapers. Cook appeared with the Eskimos in a show at Huber's Dime Museum at a salary of $300 per week, far more money than he could earn as a physician.

The public loved Cook's shows and lectures and believed he was one of America's great explorers, despite the fact that he had actually accomplished little in his own right. Cook's new dream was to lead an expedition to the Antarctic, and he hoped to raise $50,000 by capitalizing on the public's perception. To publicize the project and his role in it, he ordered stationery embossed with the words "Official Bureau of the American Antarctic Expedition. Dr. Frederick A. Cook, Commanding," implying that the expedition was sanctioned by the government or one of the well-recognized scientific societies that sometimes underwrote such expeditions.

Despite his newfound fame and his misleading and grandiose letterhead, Cook fell far short of raising the amount he needed for an Antarctic expedition. He then convinced fifty-two students and professors from various universities to pay $500 each to voyage on the steamer *Miranda* to western Greenland. Cook assured these novice explorers that the dangers of sailing in the Far North had been greatly exaggerated. These assurances proved hollow when the *Miranda* struck an iceberg north of Newfoundland. After repairs were made at St. Johns, the ship set out again but ran aground on a reef off the Greenland coast. After breaking free, it hove-to in a sheltered anchorage while Cook, surveyor Russell Porter, and three others sailed north in a lifeboat until they reached the small settlement of Holsteinborg. They informed the Danish authorities of the plight of the *Miranda,* and the governor dispatched kayaks to find one of the fishing schooners reported to be in the area. Eventually the *Rigel* rescued the *Miranda*'s passengers and crew, and they were brought back to the United States aboard other ships. Blame for the disaster fell largely on the captain and crew of the *Miranda,* although some of the passengers accused Cook of incompetent management. Most of the press, however, praised Cook's courage for facing the northern seas in a small boat.

After this fiasco, Cook had difficulty raising funds for a new expedition. In 1897 he heard that the physician for a Belgian expedition to the Antarctic was unable to make the voyage. He applied for the position and, somewhat to his astonishment, was accepted. This group of explorers soon became known as the Belgica Expedition after the vessel in which it sailed. After joining the party in Montevideo, Cook quickly made friends with the first officer, Roald Amundson, who a dozen years later would become the first person to reach the South Pole. In addition to his medical duties, Cook was the

Dr. Frederick Albert Cook, 1897

(Courtesy Byrd Polar Research Center

Archival Program)

expedition's photographer, giving him valuable experience with photographic equipment that he would later put to good use.

In the Antarctic Cook gained some climbing experience when he, Amundson, and Henryk Arctowski tried to ascend one of the peaks on Two Hummock Island, off Graham Land, by cutting steps into a vertical ice wall. In his diary, Amundson mentioned Cook's methodical nature, "It is interesting to see the practical and calm manner in which this man works." On a second attempt by a different route a few days later, Cook and Arctowski planted the American flag on the island's second highest peak. It was a relatively short climb of only a few thousand feet, but with his usual unbridled confidence Cook now fancied himself an experienced mountaineer. (In 1901 Cook and other climbing enthusiasts who accepted his premise that polar exploration and high mountain climbing are twin efforts would join together to found the American Alpine Club.)

When the *Belgica* became bound in pack ice, the expedition was forced to spend the winter in the Antarctic. During the long darkness of the polar night, Cook became the unofficial morale officer, working tirelessly to keep up the crew's spirits, while continuing to serve superbly as their physician. He earned much praise from the crew for his efforts and ingenuity. In his book, *My Life as an Explorer,* Amundson reported that: "He [Cook], of all the ship's company, was the one man of unfaltering courage, unfailing hope, endless cheerfulness, and universal kindness." Amundson's respect for Cook grew into a close friendship, which would endure until Amundson's death in 1928. In March of 1899, the *Belgica* broke free of the pack ice and returned to Europe without further incident.

Cook returned to Brooklyn and began to lecture and write rather than resuming his medical practice. His books and lecture tours were not as financially successful as he had hoped, however, and in 1901, he accepted an invitation to travel to Belgium to help organize the data from the Belgica Expedition for publication. When he returned to the United States, the Peary Arctic Club, which had been organized specifically to fund Peary's explorations in the Far North, asked Cook to be part of a rescue expedition to find Peary, who had disappeared in northern Greenland. Peary had been out of touch for so long that the club's members were growing concerned for his safety and had chartered a vessel to determine his whereabouts. Cook sailed with them to Etah on the northwestern tip of Greenland, where they found Peary ill and emaciated. After nursing him back to health, Cook returned to New York.

In 1902 Cook married Marie Fidele Hunt, a widow he had met several years before who had a young daughter named Ruth. Marie fully supported Cook's interest in exploration and saw herself accompanying her husband to remote places as Jo Peary had often done with her husband. A relatively wealthy woman in her own right, Marie also offered to help finance future expeditions.

By 1903 Frederick Cook had earned a very respectable reputation as an explorer and ethnologist. Yet in the quest for funding, he was eclipsed by Peary who had a wide variety of wealthy industrialist and socialite backers. Still, there was no open rivalry between the two. Cook kept secret his ambition of beating Peary to the North Pole, while the autocratic Peary considered Cook merely an underling. To beat Peary in the arena of financial support Cook knew he had to perform a feat so spectacular that he would be recognized as a first-rate explorer, thoroughly competent and able to lead his own polar expedition.

CHAPTER 3

Dr. Cook and Mount McKinley

Cook's interest in climbing Mount McKinley began when he read Alfred Brooks's article in the January 1903 issue of *National Geographic Magazine*. At the conclusion of the article, Brooks wrote that any expedition to Mount McKinley should "be put under the direction of a man who . . . has had long training in frontier life and exploratory work." Cook believed he was exactly such a man and that the first person to climb the highest mountain in North America would become famous enough to secure funding for an attack on the North Pole—his greatest dream. As a further bonus a trek to Alaska would cost far less than a polar expedition and would take him away from his new wife for only a few months.

Cook's naive faith in his ability to climb mountains was so great that when he examined Brooks's survey data, he thought he could easily climb 5,000 feet per day up the slopes of the almost totally uncharted mountain. To help finance his proposed climb of Mount McKinley, Cook obtained an advance from *Harper's Monthly Magazine* for a story to be written at the conclusion of the expedition. Next he approached Lincoln Steffens, the distinguished editor of the *New York Globe and Commercial Advertiser*. Steffens decided against giving Cook an advance, but he did propose that Cook take along one of his young reporters, Robert Dunn. Steffens said he would pay Dunn "double lineage" (i.e., double the usual amount per line of copy) on everything he wrote about Cook's expedition, thus guaranteeing prolific coverage. Steffens also mentioned that Dunn had a very rich aunt, Anna Hunter of Newport, who was likely to contribute generously to the expedition. Cook accepted this proposal, eager for the extra publicity that bringing a reporter with him to Alaska would provide.

Yet Steffens's proposal was not as straightforward as it seemed. Dunn was a recent graduate of Harvard who worked on the *Globe*'s "police blotter," following up on crime stories. Cynical and

antagonistic, he constantly feuded with the other reporters. "Too damned Harvard" was the comment made about him by many of his colleagues. Since Dunn was one of the *Globe*'s best reporters, Steffens did not want to fire him. By sending him to Alaska, Steffens could maintain peace among his other employees, as well as get an exciting series of stories. Steffens was the first person who felt that Cook's reputation was anything less than solid gold, confiding to Dunn that he was very suspicious of the doctor. He had no real basis for his suspicions, just the instincts of an old newspaperman. Steffens instructed Dunn to "tell the whole truth about exploring," including the rows and the bickering that he felt would surely lie ahead.

Anna Hunter gave her nephew $1,000 for his expenses in Alaska, and Dunn contributed the money to the expedition's general coffer. Cook also received $1,000 from Ralph Shainwald, a member of the Arctic Club and the son of a wealthy paint manufacturer, in exchange for a place on the expedition's roster. Cook's wife supplied the additional funds that he needed. The total budget for the expedition was approximately $5,000—a very large sum at that time. From the Peary Arctic Club, Cook also secured the loan of a compass, an aneroid barometer for measuring altitude, and a pocket sextant for measuring latitude.

Robert Dunn in 1903, during Dr. Cook's circumnavigation of Mount McKinley (Bradford Washburn collection, neg. 57-6490)

THE 1903 EXPEDITION

Cook, his wife Marie, Dunn, and Shainwald left New York for Seattle by train on May 26, 1903. There they met their horse packer, Fred Printz, who had purchased a string of ponies for the expedition from

Montana horse packer Fred Printz, year unknown (Bradford Washburn collection, neg. 57-6481)

Washington's Yakima tribe of Native Americans. Printz was an experienced frontiersman from Montana who had accompanied Alfred Brooks during his geological survey along the northern ramparts of the Alaska Range during the summer of 1902. Cook also hired Walter Miller and Jack Carroll as hands to help with the horses and equipment. The entire party boarded a steamer on its regular Inside Passage run to Alaska and landed in Tyonek on the northern shores of Cook Inlet on June 23. A few days before Cook set out for the interior, Marie went to Valdez to await his return.

For the first part of the almost 200-mile journey to the northern base of Mount McKinley, Cook split the party in two. Dunn, Shainwald, Printz, and Carroll took half the supplies overland with the horses. Cook and Miller loaded the rest of the supplies on a small boat and headed up the Susitna River to its confluence with the Yentna, then continued on to a meeting point on the Kichatna River. Poling against the current was more difficult than Cook had anticipated, and caused considerable delay. The two parties were not reunited until July 13. Cook and the others then set out to cross to the northern side of the Alaska Range on horseback. He believed, based on Brooks's observations, that an approach to Mount McKinley from the north would have the best chance for success.

The overland trek was grueling, passing through mosquito- and horsefly-infested lowlands. Several horses broke legs in hidden sinkholes. Concerning this journey, Cook later wrote, "We learned to our heart's content that this enticing landscape, so beautiful to look upon, offered us the tortures of countless devils—mosquitoes, horseflies, gnats and marshes, thick underbrush, icy streams and never-ceasing rains all combined to make us thoroughly miserable." Printz was the only member of the party with practical wilderness experience and had to shepherd the others as best he could.

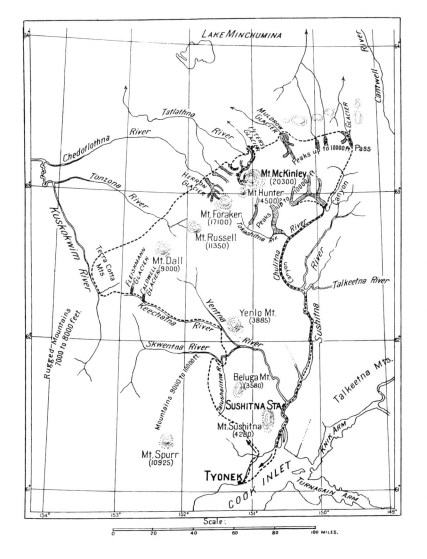

Robert Dunn's map of Dr. Cook's 1903 circumnavigation of Mount McKinley. The dotted line shows the expedition route.

Robert Dunn found that Cook totally lacked leadership skills. He was indifferent to the suffering of the packhorses, whose legs were lacerated and swollen by the thick alder underbrush. He also failed to assign members of the party specific duties and responsibilities, resulting in incessant quarreling over who should perform the regular daily chores. In an article for *Outing Magazine* based on the notes he took in Alaska, Dunn wrote: "An expedition of this sort will not lead itself, unless the leader sets an example by getting up first, starting breakfast, and leading tirelessly in every job . . . He [Cook] just fusses with his instruments." Dunn went on to say that Cook unpacked and packed a theodolite many times but never actually used it. By the end of the journey, he was convinced that Cook had little idea of the use and purpose of any of his scientific instruments.

By August 16 the expedition had reached the northern side of Mount McKinley. Time was running short. In a few weeks, the early Alaskan snows would freeze the grass on which the horses depended for fodder. After viewing the formidable 14,000-foot northern wall of the mountain, Cook settled on an approach up the Peters Glacier, heading in behind the foothills toward the West Buttress of the mountain's North Peak. At the time he was unaware that he was following the lower part of a route taken only a few weeks before by Judge James Wickersham of Fairbanks, who had just made the first attempt to scale Mount McKinley. Today, the 14,000-foot northern face is known as the Wickersham Wall.

On August 25 Cook and his team started up the glacier. Their mountaineering equipment consisted of a few ropes, sun goggles, and three ice axes. To steady themselves as they scaled slippery slopes of snow and ice, two of the climbers had to use tent poles. After four days of climbing along the easy lower part of Peters Glacier, they made camp at 7,500 feet in its upper basin after traversing its short, but particularly dangerous, icefall. Wickersham had turned back at the base of this icefall, believing that only a "flying machine" would allow a climber to ascend farther. Cook's plan was to make a rapid ascent from this point to the summit, carrying only minimal rations and equipment. He did not know that his route would have led him to the top of Mount McKinley's North Peak, which is more than 800 feet lower than the real summit located two miles to its south.

On August 29 Cook, Dunn, Shainwald, and Printz began climbing a 3,000-foot snow slope so steep that they had to cut a seemingly interminable number of steps in order to inch their way upward. By afternoon they untied the ropes binding them to each other, fearing that a slip by one person would cause the entire party to fall down the slope. Dunn was one of the unlucky members of the group who had only a tent pole to steady himself and it soon became clear to him that Cook had never before done any alpine climbing. When Dunn's turn came to lead, Cook refused to give him an ice ax, forcing him to try to bang steps in the rock-hard snow with the tent pole. Dunn later wrote that during this treacherous climb, he thought of the pitiful comments that his friends in New York would make about "this party, that with no alpine experience just butted blind into the highest mountain on the continent."

While in the lead, Dunn was the first to see a new peak just to the right of Mount McKinley, which Cook allowed him to name Mount Hunter to commemorate Anna Hunter's generous contribution to the expedition. Since the peak that we now know as Mount Hunter could not possibly have been visible from the point where they were climbing, Dunn doubtless saw the 12,000-foot Kahiltna Dome. Later surveyors assigned "Mount Hunter" to the peak that bears the name today—a magnificent 14,570-foot mountain that is a more majestic memorial to Anna Hunter than Kahiltna Dome.

The party's first camp on McKinley was a miserable one at 9,500 feet, chopped out of the steep slope they were climbing. The next day they continued upward until, at 10,800 feet, they reached a moderately level spot. Here they made a reasonably comfortable camp. The following morning, Cook and Printz scouted the terrain that lay right ahead of them. After a very short distance, they encountered a succession of steep granite ledges, which they could not possibly negotiate given their equipment and level of experience. Dunn later reported a comment by Fred Printz which summed up their predicament. "It ain't that we can't find a way that's possible, takin' chances. There ain't no way at all!" Dunn also added his own observation: "Something besides courage and determination is needed to climb a mountain like this. Forgive me if I call it intelligence." On September 2 Cook's discouraged party returned to the camp where they had left their horses. The ridge that stymied Cook would not be climbed until May 27, 1954.

Cook's failure to climb McKinley stemmed not only from the route he chose but also from his poor overall planning of the expedition. Instead of choosing experienced mountaineers as his companions, he selected a motley group based in part on their ability to pay their way. He left for Alaska late in the season and underestimated the difficulties of their northwestern approach to the mountain. His notion of making a swift dash to the summit stemmed from his experience in polar regions, where it is possible to travel swiftly over ice and glaciers. McKinley's rock-and-ice walls, however, require a full array of alpine gear and a great deal of time and competence to negotiate safely.

Rather than returning to the coast by the same route that they had come, Cook insisted that they continue eastward, hoping to find a new pass leading southward across the Alaska Range. This late in the summer, with supplies running low and horses already debilitated by insect bites and overwork, this was a very dangerous undertaking. Moving as fast as possible, on September 5 they crossed a vast gravel flat, located below today's Eielson Visitor Center in Denali National Park. That evening, near Stony Hill, they climbed a 5,000-foot mountain from which they had a marvelous view, looking westward at Mount McKinley, now barely forty miles away.

Cook described the great mountain's twin peaks, looming 15,000 feet above them, as "the tubercles of a giant tooth . . . separated by large glaciers whose frozen currents pour down very steep slopes." He then made the astute observation that "if it were not so difficult to get at this side of the mountain, here the upper slopes might offer a promising route." On his next expedition to the mountain, Cook would recall this view from Stony Hill and the opportunity it offered for an easy way to reach the summit from the northeast—in fact, the first five ascents of the great peak were all made up this side's Muldrow Glacier.

Northeast view of Mount McKinley's summit. This was the scene that prompted Cook to say " . . . from here it resembled very much the crown of a molar tooth. . . ." (neg. 3448)

For the next three days, they trekked eastward through the great valley that parallels the range—the route of today's Denali Highway—until it narrows just before reaching the East Fork of the Toklat River. By this time, their salt and tea were gone, they had cut their rations to a starvation level, and there was almost no fodder left for the horses. Cook decided they had no choice but to cross the Alaska Range by taking the next valley to the south, regardless of the obstacles it might present. By amazing luck, this turned out to be the only pass in this 140-mile span of the range across which horses could possibly be coaxed. Following the lead of Fred Printz, the party managed to work its way up a narrow

glacier with no crevasses, over a 6,000-foot pass, then down a very steep hillside to the valley of the Bull River, which leads into the upper Chulitna Valley.

Here the river was so winding that they had to cross it and recross it many times during each day's difficult trek. Dunn later wrote about their tattered condition, "Our clothes are falling to pieces, our boots are worn out; mine are a cast-off pair of [Shainwald's]." By September 16 they had reached a point where the river was too deep and swift for the horses to continue to fight their way downstream. Cook ordered his party to build rafts from cottonwood trees so they could float down the Chulitna River and into the Susitna. Their objective was Susitna Station, a trading outpost just above Cook Inlet. In another indication of his naivete about travel in the wilderness, Cook chose not to shoot the horses on which they had depended but to turn them loose to fend for themselves in the harsh wilderness, where they were sure to slowly starve to death. The next day, the expedition began rafting its way down the swift Chulitna.

Observing Mount McKinley's slopes as they passed seemed to confirm Cook's notion that a traverse from the southeast side to the northeast side was feasible. When one of the mountain's glaciers came into view, Cook called a halt in order to explore the terrain. Taking Dunn and Shainwald with him, he scouted the lower part of the glacier and called it Fidele—his new wife's maiden name. Today it is known as the Eldridge Glacier.

Farther along, they saw a second glacier, which he named Ruth, after his stepdaughter. This huge feature of Mount McKinley would play a major role in the exploration of the mountain in the years that lay immediately ahead. Returning to the rafts, they soon reached the waters of the wide Susitna River and arrived at Susitna Station without incident on September 25.

Despite his failure to climb Mount McKinley, Cook had succeeded in circumnavigating it, a remarkable feat that would not be repeated for a half century. His trek added immensely to the knowledge of the geography of that part of interior Alaska and greatly increased his reputation as an explorer. But it was not the spectacular achievement he had hoped for. His ambition to be the first to climb Mount McKinley and use the fame he derived from the exploit as a stepping-stone toward reaching the North Pole still smoldered. In the *Harper's Monthly Magazine* article that fulfilled his obligation to

The Bull River Pass. The line shows the exact route the party took over the pass. (neg. 3470)

the publisher for the advanced funds used for the expedition, he wrote: "I hope to make an attempt from the east . . . It is an effort which, for insurmountable difficulties and hard disappointments, is comparable with the task of expeditions to reach the North Pole." Dr. Cook wanted to make sure his audience recognized that the two achievements should be closely linked.

After Cook's return to New York, he gave lectures about the expedition to the Arctic Club and other groups interested in exploration and climbing, presenting excellent slides of his photographs of Mount McKinley and the Alaskan interior. But scandal soon dogged his efforts as a series of articles written by Dunn and sharply critical of Cook's leadership ability appeared in *Outing Magazine*. Outraged over Dunn's attack on Cook, members of the Arctic Club made a motion to expel him, but Cook, acting the part of an aggrieved gentleman, defended Dunn before a committee of the Club, enhancing Cook's reputation for fair play. Nonetheless, Dunn's name was removed from the Club's roster.

In 1904 Cook gave a lecture to the Canadian Camp, a group of mountaineering enthusiasts. In the audience was Dr. Herschel C. Parker, a wealthy physics professor from Columbia University, who had taken up mountaineering to strengthen his body. After the lecture, Parker took Cook aside and pledged to contribute $2,000 to another attempt to climb Mount McKinley if Cook would include him as a member of the expedition. Cook agreed and outlined a plan to take a specially designed powerboat up the rivers leading to the mountain in order to shorten the time it would take to arrive at a meeting point with packhorses traveling overland.

In 1905 Cook joined with Parker and five others to found the Explorers Club. The club attracted influential explorers and patrons such as Robert Peary and Herbert Bridgman and it rapidly became one of America's most influential organizations for supporting and evaluating exploration. Because of his reputation for competence and trustworthiness, Cook was elected president of the club in 1906.

THE 1906 EXPEDITION

After the organization of the Explorers Club, financial support for Cook's second attempt to climb Mount McKinley was quick in coming. As he had done in 1903, he secured an advance from *Harper's*

Dr. Frederick A. Cook during his 1906 expedition (Courtesy Byrd Polar Research Center Archival Program)

Monthly Magazine for a story about his intended climb. According to a record of the transaction kept by Harper and Brothers, the amount of the advance was $1,000. Cook, however, in his typical self-aggrandizing fashion later told members of the expedition that the advance was $25,000. He then approached Henry Disston, heir to a saw-manufacturing fortune. Disston agreed to contribute $10,000 to the expedition if Cook would agree to join him after his ascent of Mount McKinley for an autumn big-game hunt on the southern approaches of the Alaska Range. The *Harper's* advance, Disston's promised grant, and Herschel Parker's contribution amounted to $13,000, a sum far in excess of the $4,000 to $5,000 that such an expedition would normally cost. Cook now turned his attention to assembling a competent group to accompany him that would cause less trouble than Robert Dunn had three years before.

Parker wanted to bring his friend, Belmore Browne, an artist and outdoorsman who had recently graduated from Harvard. Cook agreed. Despite Parker's financial contribution to the expedition, he and Browne considered themselves "separate" from Cook's entourage. Cook asked Russell Porter—his companion from the *Miranda* rescue—to accompany him as the party's surveyor. He also asked Walter Miller and Fred Printz, both veterans of the 1903 expedition, to act as photographer and to handle the packhorses, respectively. Printz agreed as long as he could bring with him an assistant horse packer named Ed Barrill, a forty-year-old, two-hundred-pound, blacksmith from Darby, Montana. Barrill was powerfully built and a competent outdoorsman, but he had no mountaineering or glacier-travel experience whatsoever.

On May 16, 1906, the party sailed from Seattle. With them was a specially built power launch that was intended to run supplies up the Susitna River and which Cook called the *Bolshoy*—after the

Belmore Browne, 1945 (Courtesy Rauner Special collections, Dartmouth College Library)

early Russian settlers' name for Mount McKinley, Bolshaia Gora. This boat had a shallow draft to reduce the difficulties of navigating up the shallow and muddy Alaskan rivers. The expedition arrived in Tyonek on May 29. A few days later, as he had in the 1903 expedition, Cook split the party. Printz and Barrill led the packhorses directly northward through swampy terrain, while Cook and the others rode the *Bolshoy* up the Susitna River. The two parties then rejoined and began to search for a shorter way up the Yentna River and across the Alaska Range to the northern side of Mount McKinley, in order to make the southeast to northeast traverse that had seemed to Cook like the obvious approach after his 1903 expedition. After several wasted weeks and a frustrating and futile struggle to get the horses across a rugged pass at the head of the Yentna, Cook apparently reconsidered his plan to approach the mountain from the northeast and decided that the southeast side might indeed prove easier to negotiate. But while trekking southeastward after abandoning the Yentna approach, the party encountered swollen streams, steep slopes, and nearly impassible swamps between the Yentna and the Tokositna Rivers. Especially problematic was the creek coming out of today's Kahiltna Glacier, which was extremely difficult to ford.

By July 19 the exhausted party was camped on a high ridge above the Tokositna Valley, where they had an unobstructed view of the southeast side of Mount McKinley. Cook and Belmore Browne kept an all-night vigil while the rest of the party slept. They hoped to study Mount McKinley's upper slopes for a possible route to the top at a moment when there was no cloud cover, but their elusive goal remained shrouded in mists. In his diary, Browne noted, "the Dr. has, I think, given up all hope for making the top this year."

The 1906 Cook-Parker Expedition. Left to right: Russell Porter, Edward Barrill, Frederick A. Cook, Herschel C. Parker, Belmore Browne (Bradford Washburn collection)

The next day, they crossed the lower part of Tokositna Glacier and reached a ridge much closer to the mountain, where they could see much more of the upper reaches of the Ruth Glacier than they had on their 1903 expedition. They discovered that to get out onto the surface of the Ruth, where they would have smooth going, they would have to cross a roaring, frigid stream that rushed down a narrow gorge beside the glacier—a stream far too swift for either horses or men to manage. The team spent one more day examining the mountain, then admitted defeat. The time was drawing near when Cook would have to meet Henry Disston in Tyonek for the promised big-game hunt so they had to begin their return journey toward Tyonek. Once again, the expedition split up, with Russell Porter staying behind to map Mount McKinley's southeastern approaches as best he could. When Cook and the others reached the point where they had left the *Bolshoy,* Cook told Ed Barrill and John Dokkin, a prospector who Cook had recently hired from a mining camp they had encountered on their trek, to stay there with the horses

Edward Barrill, 1941 (Courtesy Byrd Polar Research Center Archival Program)

to prepare for the hunt with Disston. Cook and the others sped downriver to the coast in the power launch that had performed so well at the beginning of their journey.

At Tyonek, Herschel Parker boarded a steamer to return to New York in time to resume his teaching duties at Columbia University. In preparation for the hunt with Disston, Cook rented additional horses to replace the ones which had died or wandered off during their journey. A few days later on August 25, he received a telegram from Disston announcing that he would not be going to Alaska at all and that the hunt was canceled. This news prompted a major change in Cook's plans. Exactly what he intended to do was not immediately clear. Prior to leaving Tyonek, he sent a telegram to Herbert Bridgman indicating that he intended "to wire you [Bridgman] from Seward about our work early in October. If the telegram is of sufficient importance, give it to the Associated Press." In addition to this cryptic message, Cook also sent a telegram to Herschel Parker aboard ship saying that he had decided to explore the southern foothills of Mount McKinley in hope of finding a route for another attempt on the mountain the following year. Dr. Cook then broke up the remaining members of the expedition. When Belmore Browne learned of Cook's plan to explore further, he asked if he could go along. Cook emphatically refused, instead sending Browne up the Matanuska River to gather game specimens for Disston. He then took Fred Printz and Walter Miller back up the Susitna River in the *Bolshoy* to the place where Ed Barrill was waiting with the party's original horses. After meeting up with Barrill, he sent Printz and Miller into the wilderness to hunt for game to send to Disston as trophies.

Now with just Barrill and Dokkin to accompany him, Cook set off once again for further exploration of the southeastern approaches of Mount McKinley.

COOK'S CLAIM TO HAVE REACHED THE SUMMIT

Less than three weeks later, on September 22, Cook and Ed Barrill returned to Susitna Station on the *Bolshoy*. John Dokkin had remained behind in an abandoned cabin near the end of the Ruth Glacier to continue prospecting. Russell Porter joined Cook and Barrill the next day, having returned from his mapping trek. In his *Arctic Diary,* Porter wrote that upon his arrival Barrill told him to "congratulate the Doctor. He got to the top." Cook then described approaching the mountain from the Ruth Glacier and making "a hair-raising dash to the very summit . . . digging into the very face of vertical ice walls when night overtook them. The account was all very thrilling." Porter eventually made several illustrations based on Cook's description of the climb, which were later used in Cook's book *To the Top of the Continent*.

Cook, Barrill, and Porter then took the launch to Kenai, where Cook sent Herbert Bridgman the telegram of "sufficient importance" that he had promised to send in August. It read: "We have reached the summit of Mount McKinley by a new route in the north." This mention of a northerly route was the first of many discrepancies in Cook's subsequent accounts of his activities in September 1906. When relating his story to Porter, he said he approached the mountain from the Ruth Glacier, that is, from the southeast. After receiving this telegram, Bridgman informed Herschel Parker and other members of the Explorers Club, who met in an all-night session to evaluate the scant information they had on Cook's alleged achievement. Parker believed that the message from Bridgman had to be incorrect because it implied that Cook had climbed the mountain from the north side. From firsthand experience, he knew it was impossible for Cook to have crossed the Alaska Range to make a northerly approach in the short time that had elapsed since Parker himself had left Tyonek. He also cited the telegram which Cook had sent to him in August stating that he was intending only to explore the southern region. The Alpine Club members agreed to temporarily hold their judgment in abeyance and wait for additional information from Cook when he returned to New York.

When Belmore Browne finished gathering specimens and returned to Seldovia, he heard the rumors that Cook had made the ascent of Mount McKinley in only twelve days—eight days up and four to descend. His first reaction was that this was as absurd as "a man to report that he had walked the distance from Brooklyn Bridge to Grant's Tomb [a distance of 10.8 miles] in ten minutes." Browne's skepticism was further fueled after Cook and Barrill arrived in Seldovia. Browne took Barrill aside and asked him what had happened on the mountain. Barrill replied, "I can tell you all about the big peaks just south of the mountain, but if you want to know about Mount McKinley, go and ask Cook." Browne did as Barrill suggested, listening carefully to Cook's description of the climb.

Cook told Browne that he, Barrill, and Dokkin had started up the mountain from a base camp 1,000 feet above sea level at the point where Alder Creek flows into the Tokositna River. They followed the pleasant course of Alder Creek for the first five miles, then continued for several more miles along the narrow valley beside the eastern edge of the Ruth Glacier. They made camp near the big bend of the Ruth. On the afternoon of the second day, they took to the ice, crossing the first northern tributary of the Ruth. Here Dokkin became so scared of the crevasses that he returned alone to the base camp. He carried back one of Cook's three aneroid barometers with instructions to read it daily, so that Cook could later compare these readings with the readings he would take with his own barometers as he climbed the mountain. Such comparisons would allow Cook to determine the altitude he had reached with a high degree of accuracy.

The circle marks Dr. Cook and Ed Barrill's highest camp, at Alder Creek. Dr. Cook thought this camp was at an altitude of 1,000 feet, but the actual altitude is 600 feet. Alder Creek is at left and the Tokositna River is at right. (neg. 57-6566)

Cook and Barrill made their next camp on the ice near 3,800-foot Glacier Point in the middle of a stunning wilderness of rock and ice. The next day was spent investigating the region to the northeast—visiting the site of Cook's "15,400 foot" photo and the summit of what later became known as the "Fake Peak." They spent that night on moss-carpeted Glacier Point. The next day they avoided the impassable Ruth Icefall by following the glacier's eastern lateral moraine for a couple of miles. The surface of the ice then became smooth again, and they could move safely upward in the middle of the glacier without encountering any large crevasses. They then encountered the Great Gorge of the Ruth Glacier—a mile-wide river of ice nearly 4,000 feet thick, flanked by the granite cliffs of 9,600-foot Mount Dickey on the left and the 10,000-foot Mooses Tooth on the right. At noon, since a down-glacier breeze made it too cold for them to rest and lunch in the open, they pitched their tent in the middle of the smooth, crevasse-less ice. In the afternoon, they reached the upper gateway, or head, of the Great Gorge, four miles below the 10,600-foot divide between the Ruth and Traleika Glaciers.

At this point, the topographic detail in Cook's description became increasingly vague. He continued telling a tale of harrowing escapes, a night spent in a hole dug into a nearly vertical ice slope at 14,000 feet, and the dizziness he experienced at high altitude as they reached the "Heaven-scraped granite of the top." He claimed that he and Barrill had finally reached the summit, spending about twenty minutes on the highest spot in North America before beginning their extraordinary four-day descent.

After listening to Cook's tale of endurance and perseverance on the slopes of Mount McKinley, Browne temporarily put aside his doubts, impatiently waiting for the photographs and detailed descriptions that would tell the full story of the climb. Cook's relentless critic Robert Dunn was returning from a cruise to explore the lofty volcanoes of Kamchatka when the ship on which he was traveling stopped briefly in Seldovia to pick up passengers and freight for Seattle. Cook was one of the new passengers. Dunn's response to Cook's story was initially to accept the claim at face value. In a *New York Times* article appearing on October 31, 1906, he wrote: "in the course of a conversation, Dr. Cook told me that by unexpected luck, after he had practically given up hope of climbing Mount McKinley, he had, accompanied by a single packer, succeeded in reaching the summit of the peak from the northeast side . . . I do not understand why the authenticity of Dr. Cook's dispatch from Tyonek would ever have been questioned." Dunn had major doubts but lacked the solid evidence to challenge Cook's veracity. In a letter made public after his death, Dunn wrote "Cook came on board the ship to Seattle in Cook Inlet, fresh from his McKinley climb. I then questioned him on the route he took, but his answers made no sense, dropped the subject."

Thus, in October of 1906, the world believed that Dr. Frederick A. Cook and Ed Barrill had reached the top of the American continent.

CHAPTER 4

The Triumphant Hero

After Cook announced that he had reached the summit of Mount McKinley, he immediately became an American hero. He was front-page news, and the public clamored for stories about his exploits. Lecture clubs and vaudeville shows began vying to host an appearance by Cook, so he could tell the details of his harrowing adventures. Even filmmakers in the embryonic motion picture industry hastily made documentaries from stock Alaskan footage to capitalize on his sudden fame. The daring and relentless courage implicit in the few details of his climb that Cook made public captured the imagination of Americans as few events had before.

Cook, however, could not immediately leave Alaska to bask in this public adulation. He was being sued by Bill Hughes, the owner of the horses Cook had rented to replace those lost on the first part of the expedition. Cook still owed Hughes the rental fee of $600 (twenty days use at $30 a day).

The case was heard in a Seldovia court on October 25, 1906. Cook presented as his legal defense the rather novel theory that there was no contract, but rather a "provisional agreement," and even if there was a contract, it should not be enforced because the horses had not been used for the purpose Cook had originally intended, i.e., for a big-game hunt. The judge ruled that this argument had no basis in fact or in law and ordered Cook to pay Hughes $600 plus $15.18 in court costs. Cook did not have the money. Henry Disston had not paid the $10,000 he had promised, believing that his failure to arrive for the hunt had relieved him of his financial obligation, and Cook had spent all the other money he and Herschel Parker had raised. The great hero now faced the embarrassment of having his belongings sold to raise the money to pay Hughes. Cook's newly won prestige as the conqueror of Mount McKinley, however, came to his rescue. Several Alaskans offered to loan him the money, one of them

Dr. Frederick A. Cook, 1912 (Courtesy Byrd Polar Research Center Archival Program)

asking for his hat, which was eventually put on display at a local fair as the hat that had been to the highest point in North America. This case of Cook's inability to meet his financial obligations did not receive much publicity and seemed to do nothing to tarnish his growing reputation.

Cook finally left Alaska, arriving in Seattle on November 7, 1906. He checked into the Butler Hotel and began giving interviews to reporters. While he was speaking with a correspondent from the *Seattle Daily News,* his wife Marie came into the room. He had had no idea she was in Seattle. Cook's debtors, and there were others besides Bill Hughes, might have been interested to learn that while Cook was stranded in Alaska unable to pay his bills, his wife had used her own substantial funds to take a grand tour of the West, arriving in Seattle in time for Cook's return.

On November 9, Cook gave his first public talk. He spoke in Seattle to the local members of the Mazamas, a mountaineering club based in Portland, Oregon. The audience was packed with five hundred admirers who cheered and applauded Cook with the enthusiasm reserved only for national heroes.

It was in this address that Cook first described his climbing technique and the specifics of his equipment. Cook claimed that he and Ed Barrill made rapid marches carrying light, fifty-pound packs, which contained all they would need to climb the mountain in a dozen days. Cook stated that they carried a one-pound horsehair rope, a silk tent, an alcohol stove, two thermometers, three aneroid barometers, a large-format camera with six film packs, and a rubber floor cloth for their tent. Their food was pemmican, dried meat and fat pounded into a paste, which Cook had become familiar with in the Arctic. To keep warm in the sub-zero temperatures near the summit, he said they wore lightweight underwear with a flannel shirt and wool trousers. Cook claimed that their thin rubber "shoepacks" provided them with more than enough traction on the near-vertical ice slopes they had scaled. (These "shoepacks" are the equivalent of L.L. Bean's modern-day hunting shoes with rubber soles and leather uppers.)

The members of the Mazamas initially accepted Cook's version of the climb. They trusted that his as-yet-unseen photographs and other evidence would support his statements. Since at this point, no one but Cook had seen the upper reaches of Mount McKinley (except, of course, for Ed Barrill, but he was neither a climber nor an explorer, just a blacksmith from Montana), Cook's description was considered authoritative and was not questioned.

Cook returned to New York on November 27. He immediately met with Herschel Parker to explain why he had changed his mind about making another try to climb Mount McKinley after telegraphing that he was finished for the season. Parker evidently accepted Cook's explanation that the opportunity presented by the unexpected discovery of a route to the summit could not be passed up. He made no further public statements rejecting Cook's claim to have reached the summit, but he did mention to reporters that the climb was simply a feat of endurance that was of very little value to science. On December 7, Cook lectured at the Explorers Club, repeating what he had told the Mazamas. The membership was so impressed with his achievement that they speedily elected him to succeed General Adolphus Greely as president of the Club.

A week later at the National Geographic Society's annual dinner, where Robert E. Peary was the guest of honor, Cook managed to steal the limelight. The December dinner was one of the social events of the pre-Christmas season in Washington, attended by senators, congressmen, and industrialists, as well as President Theodore Roosevelt. Toward the end of the evening, after many toasts and speeches, Alexander Graham Bell rose to introduce the society's special guest—Dr. Frederick A. Cook. Bell said that Cook was a man known by name to everyone present. He went on to praise Cook as the only American who had explored both the Arctic and the Antarctic, and who now had added to his honors by reaching the top of the North American continent. He invited Cook to say a few words about his achievement. Always conscious of the value of cultivating his image as a gentleman in public gatherings, Cook managed to praise Peary rather than speak at length of his climb. He claimed that his success on the mountain was due largely to the equipment developed by polar explorers and pioneered by Peary. Since there was as yet no published account of his climb, no one in this audience could know that the equipment Cook actually used was so primitive and that only his pemmican could be seen as particularly polar in origin.

Cook's triumph was now complete. He had been acknowledged by all as the conqueror of Mount McKinley, a man with courage and abilities equal to that of his rival, Peary. But time for him to reach the North Pole was running short. Peary was preparing for another expedition to try for the Pole early in 1907. In addition, there were rumors that a motorized assault on the Pole would soon be made by other explorers, as unlikely as this might seem given the unreliability of early twentieth-century gas-fired engines. To remain in the race, Cook quickly had to find a backer of substantial means who would finance his expedition.

Cook's financial savior soon appeared in the form of John R. Bradley, the owner of a gambling house in Palm Beach, which was notorious for allowing women at its gaming tables. Bradley had begun as a faro dealer in New Orleans, working his way up to casino owner by staying one step ahead of the law and growing wealthy enough to indulge his passion for big-game hunting. Cook had met Bradley at the Arctic Club in 1905 and suggested that they hunt together for walrus and polar bear in the Arctic. After Cook's return from Alaska, Bradley decided that he and Cook should go to Greenland for this hunt. After the outfitting of a ship for the hunt in Gloucester, Massachusetts, was well underway, Cook revealed to Bradley his plan to use their trip as a launching pad for a bid to reach the North Pole. Bradley promptly wrote out a check for $10,000, and Cook began planning for an expedition to begin in July 1907.

Known to only a few was the shameful fact that Cook had still not paid some of the debts he owed for his 1906 expedition. Among those he had not paid were Ed Barrill and Fred Printz for their half-year of service, as well as Russell Porter, whose $750 salary and payment for a map that he had finished while Cook and Barrill were on the mountain, and which Cook planned to sell to the National Geographic Society, were still outstanding. As Cook prepared to leave for the North Pole, Barrill, Printz, and Porter had only his promises that the debts would eventually be paid. Perhaps Cook, having benefited from his position as the conqueror of Mount McKinley in settling the Alaska lawsuit, now trusted that his fame would squelch any scandal if the claims against him were made public.

None of these complications slowed Cook down, and on July 7, 1907, he and John Bradley sailed from Gloucester, for Greenland, just two months after the first illustrated article on his McKinley climb appeared in *Harper's Monthly Magazine*.

CHAPTER 5

The Scandal Unfolds

Among the earliest doubters of Cook's claim to have climbed Mount McKinley were residents of Alaska who had no connection to mountaineering or exploration. For more than a decade, prospectors had panned for gold at Kantishna near the base of the mountain, viewing it from every angle. Familiar as they were with Mount McKinley and the surrounding terrain, they instinctively sensed that Dr. Cook's climb could not have been made in only eight days and the descent in only four. Chief among these skeptics was the Reverend Hudson Stuck, Episcopal Archdeacon of the Yukon, who lived in Nenana, a short distance down the Tanana River from Fairbanks.

Stuck was fascinated by the great mountain and had told Alfred Brooks prior to Cook's 1906 expedition that he would rather reach the mountain's summit than own the richest gold mine in Alaska. He predicted that Cook, a *cheechaco* (an outsider poorly prepared for Alaskan conditions) would again fail to reach McKinley's summit just as he had in 1903. Reverend Stuck made a $2.50 wager with Brooks that Cook would not reach a height even close to the top. When Cook announced that he had conquered McKinley, Brooks asked Stuck for the $2.50. Stuck refused to pay and, in a letter to Brooks, held to his opinion that Cook, "a prig and a vehemently suspected ass will never climb Mount McKinley." Brooks wrote back that after listening to one of Cook's lectures and seeing the photographs taken on the mountain he was convinced Cook had reached the summit. Stuck still refused to pay. He would later decide to make his own attempt on McKinley and end up playing a significant role in the ongoing controversy.

Within the mountaineering and exploration community, the earliest doubters of Cook's claim were Belmore Browne and Professor Herschel Parker. Their suspicions sprang from their firsthand knowledge of Cook's abilities and their observations while climbing in Mount McKinley's southern approaches. It was plain to them that Cook had only limited, if any, mountaineering skill. More tellingly, Browne and Parker had reconnoitered Mount McKinley thoroughly enough to know that it was a formidable adversary, unlikely to be scaled as easily or as quickly as Cook had reported. Immediately skeptical of his claims, they nevertheless tried to keep an open mind while they waited to see Cook's evidence.

A few months after Cook's return to New York, Browne and Parker attended one of his lectures, which was illustrated with lantern slides made from the photographs he had taken on the mountain but had not yet published. What they saw did not reflect their experience in the area or their expectation of seeing views unmistakably shot from high elevations. They voiced their concerns to the experienced mountaineers of the American Alpine Club, sparking a rumor that Cook had falsified his claim to have reached the mountain's summit. Cook retaliated by threatening a slander suit against Browne and Parker, who resolved to keep silent about their suspicions until all of Cook's evidence had been made public.

Cook's account of the climb finally appeared in the May 1907 issue of *Harper's Monthly Magazine*. Photos illustrated the article, including one entitled, "The Summit of Mount McKinley, 20,300 feet above sea level," which showed Ed Barrill standing on a small rocky peak, waving the American flag with footsteps in soft, fluffy snow in its foreground—the thing that one sees on peaks 5,000–6,000-feet high, but never at high altitude where fierce winds beat deep snows to windswept hardpacks. Each of the other photographs was captioned to describe the view it was supposed to represent. None of the photos showed down-angle shots of recognizable landmarks that could only have been taken from the highest elevations. Cook also included a large-scale map that vaguely depicted his route from the Susitna River, up the Ruth Glacier, across a high pass to the northeast side of the mountain, then to the summit via what is now called the Muldrow Glacier.

Now Browne and Parker had tangible evidence that they could examine closely and objectively. As they studied the photographs in the article, they grew even more convinced that Cook had lied about reaching the summit. The snow and ice conditions visible in the photographs were quite unlike those actually to be found at the altitudes at which Cook purported to have taken the pictures. Cook's captions came under further fire when Admiral Colby Chester came forward to say that following a lecture on his McKinley climb at the National Geographic Society Cook had told Chester that he had had to leave his camera and other impedimenta at the foot of the highest slope in order to manage the difficult climb.

Unfortunately, by the time Browne and Parker were prepared to confront Cook, he had already left for the Arctic. They considered bringing before the Explorers Club their charge that Cook had committed fraud but, recalling the earlier threat of a civil suit, were reluctant to challenge Cook's integrity while he was absent.

Cook was still in the Arctic when his book about the climb, *To the Top of the Continent,* was published simultaneously in New York by Doubleday Page and in London by Hodder and Stoughton. With an introduction written by the respected explorer, and Cook's predecessor in the Mount McKinley area, Alfred H. Brooks, the book also included a chapter on the natural history of the area around Mount McKinley written by Charles Sheldon, a highly respected naturalist. The prestige of these two contributors, along with a review in London's respected *Alpine Journal,* which accepted that Cook had reached the summit, gave his claim added strength.

When Browne and Parker compared the book with the *Harper's* article, they found numerous discrepancies between the two. *To the Top of the Continent* contained several of the same photos as the article, but many of the captions had been changed to make them less specific. For example, the photo identified as "The View From 16,000 Feet" in the article was now captioned "Scene of Glaciers, Peaks and Cliffs. Shoulder of Mount McKinley. A Cliff of 8,000 feet. Ruth Glacier, a freight-carrier of the Cloud World. The Great White Way, where the polar frosts meet the Pacific Drift of the tropical Dews." The most telling discrepancy, however, was the change in the picture that Cook purported to have taken of the summit.

The "summit" photo in the book shows a distant peak in the lower right-hand corner that appears to be of higher altitude than the one on which Barrill is standing. Apparently, the photograph of the summit that had appeared in *Harper's* had been cropped or retouched to remove this distant peak. Cook had been closely involved with preparing the *Harper's* article for publication, but due to his absence in the Arctic, he had left the editorial work on his book to others. When the discrepancies in the photo captions were pointed out, Cook's supporters blamed the editors at Doubleday for inserting different captions than Cook had intended. There is, however, not a scintilla of evidence indicating that Doubleday did not publish the material exactly as Cook had submitted it. Furthermore, Cook himself never claimed that there were any errors in the book.

The private doubts of Browne, Parker, and other knowledgeable mountaineers could only simmer until Cook's return from the Arctic. Not only was it ungentlemanly to challenge him in his absence, but any accusation of fraud would have to be supported by enough evidence to avoid being sued for slander as Cook had threatened. Browne and Parker convinced the Explorers Club to confront Cook with the discrepancies at the first possible opportunity, but until then the matter would be held in abeyance. They intended to get at the truth privately without creating a public outcry.

THE NORTH POLE

On September 1, 1909, the Danish Foreign Office received a telegram from a ship on which Cook was sailing from Greenland to Copenhagen. It read: "Dr. Cook reached the North Pole April 21, 1908. Arrived May 1909 at Upernivik from Cape York. The Cape Yorkers confirm to Rasmussen the voyages of Cook." Because the telegram indicated that the famous Danish explorer Knud Rasmussen supported the claim, the Danes immediately accepted Cook's story. Cook also cabled the *New York Herald,* offering exclusive rights to his story for $3,000. The *Herald* accepted and on September 2, 1909, ran a triple banner headline stating: THE NORTH POLE IS DISCOVERED BY DR. FREDERIC [sic] A. COOK WHO CABLES TO THE HERALD AN EXCLUSIVE ACCOUNT OF HOW HE SET THE AMERICAN FLAG ON THE WORLD'S TOP. The American public quickly embraced the conqueror of Mount McKinley, who had now performed an even more daring feat of exploration.

For the first few days after this news broke, the members of the Explorers Club felt that to confront Cook about his McKinley climb at this time would surely cause them to be viewed as smallminded men trying to diminish America's greatest hero. Not yet certain that he had falsified his McKinley claim, they did not even consider the possibility that he would also falsify a claim to have reached the North Pole. Then, on September 6, the controversy entered a new phase. Robert Peary sent a telegram to the newspapers from Labrador announcing that he had reached the North Pole on April 6, 1909, almost a full year after Cook claimed to have done so. The message went on to say: "Cook's story should not be taken too seriously. The two Eskimos who accompanied him say he went no distance north and not out of sight of land. Other members of the tribe corroborate their story." Initially, the American press ignored Peary's challenge to Cook's claim, believing that Peary's personal stake in discrediting Cook was too high for his word to be taken unconditionally. The evidence against Cook, however, was now beginning to build.

The *New York Sun* was the first major newspaper to suggest that Cook's Mount McKinley and North Pole claims should not be taken at face value. On September 5, a day before Peary's telegram arrived, it ran a story saying it was rumored that Herschel Parker had doubts that Cook had reached the summit of the mountain. The *Sun* also ran an interview with Fred Printz in which he stated that Cook had perpetrated a fraud, and that he and Ed Barrill had remained silent in hope of recovering the large sum of money that Cook still owed them. On September 8, Parker was so incensed by the growing hero-worship of Cook that he felt compelled to say something in public. He made no specific charges, but in a *New York Times* interview said, "A man of science quite naturally asks why he did not make photographs of the other summit of Mount McKinley, only a short distance away, and of views about him . . . I am a friend of Dr. Cook, but in matters of this kind, scientific proof is needed. If Dr. Cook has climbed Mount McKinley, then he has made a bad case of it, as the lawyers say."

At about this time, Herbert Bridgman received a letter from J. E. Shore, a U.S. Commissioner in the state of Washington who had evidence of Cook's unpaid bills to Printz, Barrill, and various Alaskans who had provided goods and services to his McKinley expedition. Bridgman passed this information on to General Thomas Hubbard, owner of the *New York Globe and Commercial Advertiser,* the same newspaper that had refused to fund Cook's Alaskan expedition in 1903. Hubbard asked an attorney from Washington named James Ashton to interview the individuals mentioned in Shore's letter. Walter Miller, who had been with Cook on both of his trips to Alaska, helped Ashton with this investigation.

They found that many of Cook's debts from the 1906 Alaska expedition still remained unpaid.

By early October newspapers had begun to print rumors that Barrill had a diary that would disprove Cook's claim to have climbed Mount McKinley. An article in the *New York Times* cited an unnamed man who had read this diary. "This man says that the book bears on its face the evidence of its authenticity. It shows its age and the usage it has had, and in the manner and matter of its contents gives every reason for belief in its truth."

Since Barrill had not yet stepped forward with his account of the Mount McKinley climb, the *Times* eagerly fanned the controversy by simultaneously running an article that attacked Barrill. "Barrille is a French-Canadian . . . he has the loquacity of his people, which has resulted in more or less skepticism around here as to the exact value of the tales he tells." (The inclusion of an extra letter in Barrill's name was derived from a misspelling in Cook's accounts; he had never taken the trouble to learn how to spell his climbing companion's name.) This was the first use of the technique of attacking an individual's ethnicity or integrity rather than examining the evidence, which eventually became the primary method used by Cook supporters to defend their hero.

Worried over rumors that Barrill would reveal what actually took place on Mount McKinley, Cook sent a telegram asking him to come to New York at once. Barrill did not reply. Cook then sent him a letter. "I am very anxious to see you to talk over the past and the future. I enclose $200 cash—and if possible would like you to meet me in St. Louis on Oct.6. I will pay all expenses and pay you liberally for the time lost. It is important that I should see you. Kindly give no press interviews whatsoever." No longer trusting Cook's promises of payment, Barrill did not go to St. Louis, nor did he reply to the letter. What happened to that two-hundred dollars is still a mystery.

Cook now tried to explain his unpaid debts. In a *New York Times* interview, he claimed, "I was not responsible for the bills, but the society that had care of the expedition must have overlooked these payments. When my attention was called to the bills, I promptly paid them." Neither statement was true. There had been no "society" either granting money to the 1906 expedition or overseeing its expenditures. The funds actually received by Cook came from *Harper's Monthly Magazine* and Herschel Parker, both private sources, and Cook was solely responsible for using this money to pay the

Guide Who Went on Alaskan Expedition Swears Alleged Discoverer of the North Pole Was Never Nearer Than Fourteen Miles of the Summit of the North American Continent's Tallest Peak—Highest Elevation Reached Not in Excess of Ten Thousand Feet.

IN AFFIDAVIT TEARS TO PIECES DR. COOK'S CLAIM

Changes Ordered in Guide's Diary to Make It Appear That the Top of the Mountain Was Attained—Viewed Peak From All Sides So As to Be Able to Write Plausible Description—How Photograph of Barrill on the "Summit" Was Made Without Exposing Its Falsity on Its Face.

(This is not copyrighted.)

Dr. Cook's claim to "the conquest of the pole having been called in question, definite proof is now offered that his earlier claim to having achieved the ascent of Mt. McKinley was without foundation. ... he ... only man who accompanied him ... high ...

The photograph opposite page 26 ... doctor's book, entitled "In the silent glory and snowy wonder of the upper world, 15,400 ft.," was taken two or three hours before the taking of my picture with the flag, and was taken in the amphitheatre about one mile North-easterly of the point where it was so photographed.

Edw. N. Barrill

Subscribed and sworn to before me this 4th day of October, 1909.

{SEAL}

Notary public in and for State of Washington, residing at Tacoma.

Facsimile of New York's Globe and Commercial Advertiser's *October 14, 1909 coverage of Edward Barrill's affidavit, including the section with Barrill's signature. (Bradford Washburn collection)*

expedition's debts. Even after the debts became public knowledge, Cook did not pay them.

Meanwhile, lawyer James Ashton was engaged in lengthy discussions with Ed Barrill urging him to disclose publicly his information about Cook's activities on Mount McKinley. At first, Barrill asked Ashton for his unpaid wages in return for full disclosure. Then, sensing that there was money to be made from his testimony, he increased his demands. On October 1 Ashton withdrew $5,000 from General Hubbard's account at the Fidelity Trust Company and gave it to Barrill. Barrill then agreed to have his diary transcribed by a stenographer and to sign an affidavit testifying to his version of what happened. On October 8, with the documents in hand, Ashton headed for New York.

A few days later, the *New York Globe and Commercial Advertiser* printed Barrill's affidavit in its entirety. Barrill swore that Cook did not reach the summit of Mount McKinley and had falsely captioned many of the photographs taken during the climb. The affidavit was accompanied by a sketch of the actual route followed by Cook and Barrill, which showed a deviation from the alleged route of over a day's duration toward the northeast and indicated that they had not climbed higher than approximately 5,000 feet. Barrill also said that the entries in his diary from September 9 through 18, 1906—the critical days when they were on Mount McKinley—were dictated to him by Cook. The affidavit further stated that Cook's signature and address appeared on the last page of the diary, proving that he knew of its existence. The affidavit agreed with the statement that Printz had given to the *Sun* a month earlier regarding Barrill's conversations with him.

When approached by journalists, Cook claimed that he was unaware that Barrill had kept a diary and that "any statement of his [Barrill's] suggesting the changing of dates and altitude is a lie." One of the newspapermen present noted, "As usual, he never once lost his self-control." Cook's supporters then began a relentless attack on Barrill, impugning his integrity and his motives. They claimed that he had been bribed by Robert Peary to commit perjury, although there is no evidence that Peary had any connection with Barrill. They pointed out that Barrill's diary contained the spelling and grammatical

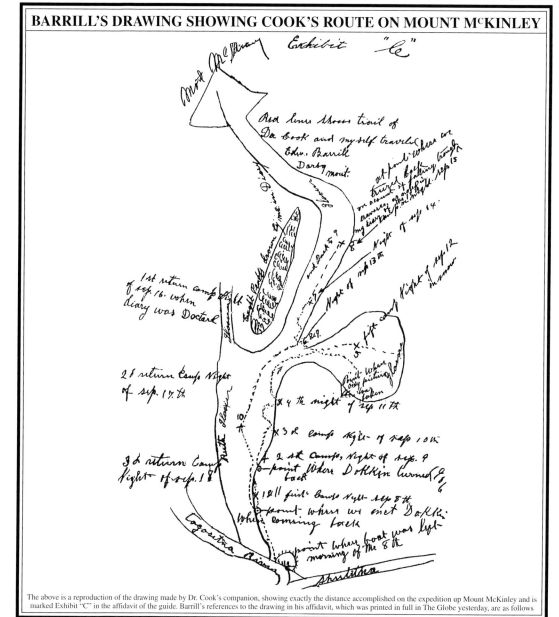

BARRILL'S DRAWING SHOWING COOK'S ROUTE ON MOUNT McKINLEY

The above is a reproduction of the drawing made by Dr. Cook's companion, showing exactly the distance accomplished on the expedition up Mount McKinley and is marked Exhibit "C" in the affidavit of the guide. Barrill's references to the drawing in his affidavit, which was printed in full in The Globe yesterday, are as follows

Edward Barrill's sketch map, published in the Globe and Commercial Advertiser *on October 15, 1909. Bradford Washburn's transcription of Edward Barrill's hand-written data is shown in the illustration on page 67. (Bradford Washburn collection)*

BARRILL'S DRAWING SHOWING COOK'S ROUTE ON MOUNT MᶜKINLEY

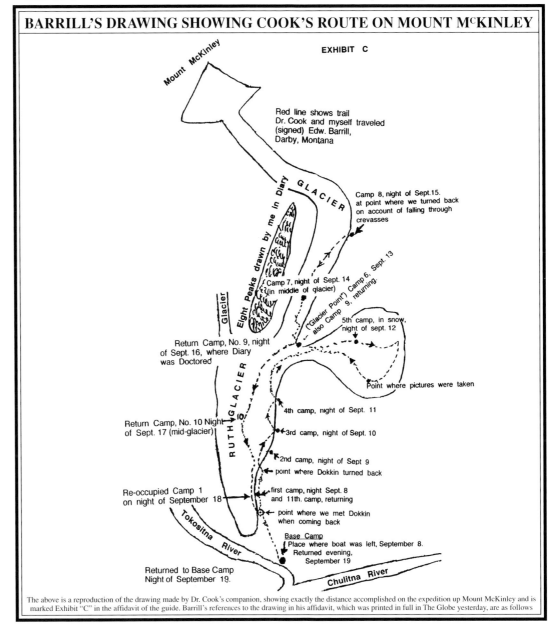

EXHIBIT C

Mount McKinley

Red line shows trail
Dr. Cook and myself traveled
(signed) Edw. Barrill,
Darby, Montana

Diary GLACIER

Eight Peaks drawn by me in Diary

Glacier

Camp 8, night of Sept.15.
at point where we turned back
on account of falling through
crevasses

Camp 7, night of Sept. 14
(in middle of glacier)

Camp 6, Sept. 13

("Glacier Point") Camp 9, returning.
also Camp 9, returning.

5th camp, in snow,
night of sept. 12

Return Camp, No. 9, night
of Sept. 16, where Diary
was Doctored

RUTH GLACIER

Point where pictures were taken

4th camp, night of Sept. 11

Return Camp, No. 10 Night
of Sept. 17 (mid-glacier)

3rd camp, night of Sept. 10

2nd camp, night of Sept 9

point where Dokkin turned back

Re-occupied Camp 1
on night of September 18

first camp, night Sept. 8
and 11th. camp, returning

point where we met Dokkin
when coming back

Tokositna River

Base Camp
Place where boat was left, September 8.
Returned evening,
September 19

Returned to Base Camp
Night of September 19.

Chulitna River

The above is a reproduction of the drawing made by Dr. Cook's companion, showing exactly the distance accomplished on the expedition up Mount McKinley and is
marked Exhibit "C" in the affidavit of the guide. Barrill's references to the drawing in his affidavit, which was printed in full in The Globe yesterday, are as follows

errors expected from a semiliterate blacksmith, not the refined prose that an educated man like Cook would dictate. Yet if Cook told Barrill what to write in general, rather than dictating specific words, Barrill would have recorded it in his own style. If Barrill's affidavit were the only evidence against Cook, it would stand as one man's word against another's. However, the diary turned out to be only one of many pieces of extraordinary new evidence accumulating against Cook.

Cook's calm demeanor in the midst of this media carnival convinced a large portion of the public that his claims should be believed. A consummate showman whose experience in lecture halls and venues such as Huber's Dime Museum had taught him how to please a crowd, Cook's enthusiasm and apparent sincerity inspired confidence. After spending an hour or two listening to him, people were certain he spoke the truth. Accepting Cook's word became an act of faith for many people. Placards and posters circulated proclaiming, "Cook, I believe in you." Much of this frenzy of unqualified adulation stemmed from the national pride of Americans.

In the autumn of 1909, the Danes and other Europeans tentatively accepted that Cook had reached the North Pole, pending the findings of the Royal Danish Commission, which would examine his evidence. All Americans would be embarrassed if the hero that the Europeans had come to respect was shown to be a charlatan. Meanwhile, Cook was profiting from the controversy by securing a number of lecture engagements that paid generous honoraria. Royalties increased from sales of *To the Top of the Continent,* and Doubleday Page ordered a second printing. The newspapers were also profiting from increased sales stimulated by the controversy and printed stories both supporting and attacking Cook's claims.

Despite Barrill's charges, the mayor of New York decided to grant Cook the "Freedom of the City of New York" on October 15. Such an honor had never before been bestowed on an American citizen. General Hubbard as well as the Explorers Club asked the mayor for a postponement until Cook's McKinley claim could be settled, but the mayor went ahead with the ceremony to please his constituents. In his acceptance speech, Cook said, "I will substantiate every claim I have made with every proof within the power of man."

Two days prior to this ceremony, Ed Barrill had arrived in New York to meet with General Hubbard and Marshall Saville, the chairman of the Explorers Club committee investigating Cook's Mount McKinley claim. Barrill repeated the same story that appeared in his affidavit, then returned to Montana. The full committee met on October 15, the same day that the affidavit was made public and that Cook announced, after conferring with his lawyer, that he too had kept a diary of the climb. Belmore Browne and Herschel Parker were the main witnesses against Cook and were at last confident enough to speak out. They discussed their suspicions, in particular those about Cook's photographs. The committee adjourned until October 17, when Cook again faced the Explorers Club committee along with his attorney, H. Wellington Wack.

Wack opened the proceedings by insisting that the committee members were prejudiced against his client and were pawns of Robert Peary, who was then president of the club. (Wack's scathing attack overlooked the fact that there were several Cook sympathizers sitting on the committee, including Henry Walsh, who had been aboard the *Miranda* on Cook's 1898 Greenland expedition; Caspar Whitney, who had pleaded for Cook to be allowed ample opportunity to present his proof; and Anthony Fiala, one of the few genuine Arctic explorers of the day.) Wack then read a prepared statement indicating that Cook needed more time to gather his material on the McKinley climb, claiming that the controversy over the climb had caught him unprepared and that "the hardships of the long Polar night had affected his memory." Wack also requested that any questions from the committee be submitted in writing so that Cook could answer them when he returned from a lecture tour to several western states. The committee agreed. When Cook asked for clarification as to what the committee expected in support of his claim, they requested the original diary, any unpublished photographs of the climb, and the negatives of the pictures that had appeared in *To the Top of the Continent*. Cook promised to provide the requested proof and answer all questions as soon as he returned.

On October 28, as part of his western lecture tour, Cook spoke in Hamilton, Montana, a town close to the place where both Fred Printz and Ed Barrill lived. Referring to the artifacts he supposedly had left on Mount McKinley, he told the crowd, "My records are on the summit of the Alaskan peak, and, accompanied by unbiased, fair-minded men, I pledge you my word that I will again reach the top of the mountain and bring back this unquestionable proof of the success of my former expedition."

The audience, however, no longer credited Cook's word. With catcalls and jeers, it insisted that he confront Barrill and Printz who were watching from the back of the hall. Barrill stood and repeated the statements in his affidavit. Cook continued to assert that they had made it to the summit but did not refute Barrill's specific points. Then he accused Barrill and Printz of taking bribes. After Cook left the lecture hall, the audience voted to affirm their faith in Barrill and Printz.

This confrontation was such an unpleasant experience for Cook that he sequestered himself from the public. Rumors flew that he had suffered a nervous breakdown. The question of his whereabouts became front-page news, with one newspaper offering a $1,000 reward for information as to his location. Wellington Wack explained that he was in seclusion to protect himself from his enemies and hinted that Robert Peary and his associates were plotting to steal the documents that would prove Cook had made it to the North Pole. Wack confirmed that Cook was hiding in a European hotel with the windows to his room nailed shut, believing that he was being shadowed by as many as six detectives bent upon snatching his documents. By November 28 the *New York Times* had had enough of this contrived comic opera and ran an article asking, "Has Cook started on a dash to the south pole, or to the north pole, or to Mars, or has he dashed anywhere? It is all a mystery."

On December 7 George Dunkle and August Loose signed affidavits swearing Cook had hired them after his North Pole expedition to create a believable set of latitude and longitude readings that would support his story of traveling to the pole. Cook initially gave them $260 for their services with a promise of $1,500 more if the readings were accepted by the Danish scientists reviewing Cook's claim to have reached the Pole. These affidavits caused the Danish commission charged with verifying the polar claim to carefully examine all of Cook's original field data. Cook had submitted a typed folio of the articles he had written for the *New York Herald,* a handwritten copy of his notebook, and the results of astronomical observations without the underlying original sighting data. On December 21, 1909, the Danish Royal Commission ruled against Cook, stating that the material submitted "does not contain observations or information which could be considered to prove that Dr. Cook had reached the Northpole [sic] on his last polar trip."

Cook now stayed away from the public for ten months. Although newspapers reported that he had been sighted in various cities from Jerusalem to Caracas, he was actually in Europe. In September of 1910, the *New York Times* ran a report of a Cook sighting. He was enjoying himself in Munich, where he "wandered about in the lobby of the hotel, the most unconcerned person in it." The disappearance worked to Cook's advantage. The public became even more fascinated by this enigmatic man and was now more eager than before to pay to hear him lecture. Had Cook directly faced his critics and their demands for evidence, perhaps he would have been quickly discredited and forgotten, his earning power as a controversial explorer forever shattered.

As it was, Cook's word still carried great weight with the general public. As testimony to the public's continued faith in him, merchants reported that the sale of Cook dolls and other memorabilia—which had slumped as the scandal broke just before Christmas of 1909—had again grown briskly. In straw polls conducted by newspapers, the public ignored his lack of supporting evidence and the considered judgment of his colleagues. By wide margins, they affirmed their belief that Cook had climbed Mount McKinley and had also reached the North Pole.

Although Cook had failed to adequately prove his claims, as far as his supporters were concerned this was not the same as *disproving* that he had climbed Mount McKinley or reached the North Pole. This reliance on faith rather than fact was infuriating to individuals like Belmore Browne and Herschel Parker, who were accustomed to evaluating data by the standards of scientific methodology. Polar exploration was not their area of expertise, but they resolved to make whatever effort necessary to at least disprove Cook's Mount McKinley claim. This required that they discover the locations where he had taken each of his photos and match his descriptions against the actual conditions found on the mountain. This would prove no easy task on the uncharted mountain.

FOLLOWING COOK'S TRAIL

While Cook hid from his critics, the Explorers Club waited in vain for the proof that he had promised. On December 28, 1909, the club grew weary of his continued silence and dropped Cook from their role of members. The following day, the American Alpine Club also removed him from its membership roles but indicated a willingness to reverse this decision if he provided details of the McKinley climb before March 1, 1910. Dr. Cook never produced these details and was thus removed from the club's membership.

General Hubbard suggested that the Explorers Club send an expedition to Mount McKinley to find utterly convincing evidence that would expose Cook's fraud. The club members agreed and asked Browne and Parker to lead such an expedition. Herbert Bridgman, rankled to think he might have supported a charlatan, pledged $3,000 toward its expenses. The purpose of this climb was not to reach the summit but to precisely follow Cook's alleged route, take photographs from the same places where he had taken the pictures for his *Harper's* article and his book, and determine beyond question how far he and Barrill actually did climb.

Unknown to the members of the Explorers Club, at the same time that they were deliberating about a course of action, four prospectors left Fairbanks intending to climb Mount McKinley. This expedition had been conceived in October when news of Barrill's affidavit arrived in Alaska. Tom Lloyd, an overweight man in his fifties, had stood in Bill McPhee's saloon bragging that a real Alaskan sourdough should plant a flag on the summit of the mountain that could be clearly seen all the way from Fairbanks. McPhee offered to pay Lloyd $500 to make a climb, a sum matched by two other merchants. They also said Lloyd would receive an additional $5,000 if he could reach the summit before July 4.

Lloyd accepted the offer and selected three other prospectors—Pete Anderson, Charlie McGonagall, and Billy Taylor—to accompany him. The four were accustomed to winter travel by dog team and made their first camp in the foothills of Mount McKinley on February 27, 1910. Nothing further was heard from them until April 11, when Lloyd strode into McPhee's saloon to announce that all four members of his climbing team had made it to the top. He declared that the summit of Mount McKinley was covered with packed snow and bore no resemblance whatsoever to Cook's photograph or the florid description of granite pinnacles included in both the *Harper's Monthly* article and Cook's book. Lloyd also explained that the other members of the party had stayed behind in the Kantishna district to work their mining claims but would return to Fairbanks after a few weeks. His

Facing page: The Sourdough team that made the first ascent of Mount McKinley's North Peak in the spring of 1910. They left a pole on the peak, which members of the Hudson Stuck party saw in 1913. Left to right: Charley McGonagall, Pete Anderson, Tom Lloyd (seated), and Billy Taylor. (Courtesy University of Alaska, Rasmuson Library, Fairbanks, Alaska)

photographs of the climb, however, were so poorly shot that they were unsatisfactory as real proof of what had been done. His claim was immediately challenged as a fraudulent attempt to collect the $5,000 promised by the Fairbanks merchants.

In response to this charge, Lloyd sent a message to the other three members of his party, who were still at their mining claims, telling them to climb the mountain again. On June 9 the *Fairbanks Daily Times* ran an article, dictated by Lloyd, stating that the three had climbed Mount McKinley a second time. The so-called Sourdough climbers claimed to have found a flag they had planted at the summit on their first climb. The story went on to say, "They believe that the Belmore Browne party will have no trouble finding their stakes." The photographic proof from this climb was as unconvincing as that from the first climb, and few people believed their story.

On May 26, 1910, while the Alaskans were making their climb, the expedition led by Belmore Browne and Herschel Parker arrived at Susitna Station. They intended to use the little sketch-map that had accompanied Ed Barrill's affidavit as the starting point for their research. In the four years since they had last been there Susitna Station had grown from a tiny outpost into a village, and, just by chance, they encountered another party, sponsored by the Mazamas of Portland, Oregon, heading for Mount McKinley. Cook's appearance before the club in 1906 had resulted in beneficial publicity that had brought in many new members, and the Mazamas, including the leader of the expedition, Claude Rusk, were very sympathetic to his claim.

The two parties had very different objectives. Rusk and his three companions were intent on proving Cook's route by using it to reach the summit. Browne and Parker also planned to retrace Cook's route,

but they were primarily intent on identifying the locations where Cook had shot his photographs in order to disprove all of his claims. Both groups recognized that while there might never be enough objective proof to settle Cook's polar claim one way or the other, plenty of evidence could be gleaned from the mountain itself to either support or disprove his McKinley claim. The two parties proceeded independently up the Susitna River to Talkeetna, up the Chulitna River to the Tokositna, then about a mile up the Tokositna to its confluence with tiny Alder Creek. This was where Cook had positioned his base camp, just below the end of the Ruth Glacier and at an altitude of only 600 feet above sea level. Browne and Parker used a motor launch to navigate the rivers, arriving at Alder Creek well ahead of the Mazamas, who traveled overland. Unlike Cook and Barrill who had carried only light packs, both parties were heavily equipped and were prepared to stay in the field the entire summer if necessary.

Browne and Parker proceeded up the Ruth Glacier along its eastern edge. At the lower turn of the Ruth, they went out onto the ice until they reached the Ruth Icefall. Since this icefall could not be

Members of the Browne-Parker expedition, July 1910. From left to right: Valdemar Frassi, J.H. Cuntz, Merl LaVoy, Herman L. Tucker, and Herschel C. Parker. (Courtesy Rauner Special collections, Dartmouth College Library)

climbed, they hiked up to the grassy crest of Glacier Point at 3,800 feet, just as Cook had done. This crest, described by Cook as "a green oasis in a desert of rock and ice," was the last spot where it was possible to camp on dry land. At this point, Browne and Parker, still well ahead of the Mazamas, deviated from Cook's route by following Barrill's map. They traveled several miles northeast in the direction that Barrill had indicated was the actual path taken on the 1906 climb.

For Browne and Parker, the first order of business was to locate the peak that Cook had claimed was the summit of Mount McKinley. After spending a comfortable night at Glacier Point, they descended to the glacier once more and turned up a side glacier that led to a low pass. As they climbed this glacier, they soon saw several small granite peaks to the right. One of these had a large vertical rock cliff to its right and thus looked very much like the "summit" depicted in Cook's photograph. They easily climbed directly to the top of this peak, which stood a mere 500 feet above the glacier. When they reached its tiny summit, they were thrilled to see a view that was identical to the photo labeled "View from 16,000 feet" that Cook had published in *Harper's Monthly Magazine*. Browne named the location the Fake Peak. The current GPS altitude of this position is 5,386 feet. This was a very exciting discovery because it confirmed that Barrill had told the truth in his affidavit when he maintained that he and Cook had gone no higher than approximately 5,000 feet.

Unfortunately, at this time of year an exact duplicate of Cook's photo could not be made. Cook had taken his pictures in mid-September when the snow had melted enough to expose the rocky ledges of the peak, and there was only a small amount of fresh, fluffy snow in the foreground of his photo. When Browne and Parker reached the peak on June 28, the top was still deeply covered with snow, and much of its detail was concealed from view. Nonetheless, Browne was able to get an excellent photo that showed enough exposed granite on its right edge for them to be certain they were on the exact spot where Cook had taken his "summit" photo. Browne later wrote, "Our mountain detective work was based on the fact that no man can lie topographically. In all the mountain ranges of the world, there are no two hillocks exactly alike."

Meanwhile, the Mazamas had begun their climb, following Cook's route to Glacier Point as Browne and Parker had done. Although Claude Rusk was well disposed toward Cook's claim, he could not help noting the discrepancies between Cook's assertions and his own observations. Cook claimed that he had mapped out a route by which to ascend the mountain while viewing it from the Chulitna River. In an article appearing in the October 1910 issue of *Pacific Monthly,* Rusk wrote: "This is absurd. Mount McKinley can be seen from a number of points along the Chulitna; but the distance is so great (about 50 miles) and the intervening mountains are so high that any man who speaks of mapping a practicable route of ascent from any of these points either exposes his ignorance of mountaineering or attempts to work upon the credulity of his readers."

As they followed Cook's trail, the climb was arduous, but for Rusk and his party, who were experienced mountaineers, it was just a long hike. Avoiding the Ruth Icefall by climbing Glacier Point, they then moved up the smooth and easily traversed upper valley of the Ruth (known today as the Great Gorge of the Ruth), which is flanked on both sides by mile-high granite cliffs. Rusk quickly determined that this was the point where Cook's map and text departed from reality. When they reached the Ruth Amphitheater (now known as the Sheldon Amphitheater) at 5,000 feet, it was obvious to them that Cook and Barrill had not climbed much farther than this point. In his *Pacific Monthly* article, Rusk wrote: "We were here, perhaps within nine miles of the summit in a straight line; but they were *miles that no man could travel.* We soon saw that the ascent from this point was impossible; although I believe the southwest ridge of the mountain may be reached from this route." (The southwest ridge was indeed eventually climbed from the Sheldon Amphitheater, but not until 1954.)

On July 12, at the edge of the Sheldon Amphitheater, the Mazamas encountered Browne and Parker, who shared their discoveries with them. Rusk and the other members of his party now had no doubt that Cook's claim was false. In his *Pacific Monthly* article, Rusk also pointed out that they had come close enough to see that the summit was "capped by an immense dome of snow . . . whereas when Cook was there, it was nearly bare." He also identified the spot beyond which he believed Cook did not go: "Cook and Barrill seem to have reached a point on Ruth Glacier about abreast of Peak Seven [today's Mount Barrill, 7,630 feet]. The book shows no picture beyond that place. Had Cook gone farther, he surely would never have neglected to secure photographs of the wonderful panorama that unfolds itself around the head of the glacier." It was indeed at this point on the glacier that, according to Barrill, they had turned back. By the end of his climb, Rusk had become "thoroughly disillusioned with Cook."

On July 15, at an altitude of 5,000 feet and with the summit of Mount McKinley towering three vertical miles above them, the Mazamas abandoned their attempt to find a route to the top and returned to civilization. Herschel Parker and Belmore Browne remained on the mountain for another two weeks, exploring as high as 10,000 feet at the very head of the western fork of the Ruth Glacier and taking many additional photographs. Prior to departing, they returned to the Fake Peak, where some snowmelt had occurred but still not enough to fully expose its granite ledges.

Browne, Parker, Rusk, and the others involved with the Mazamas and the Explorers Club expeditions returned home and rather triumphantly reported that the data they had gathered was more than enough to expose Cook's hoax. But to their surprise, instead of being hailed as objective and thorough investigators, they were attacked by Cook's supporters—who simply ignored this flood of indisputable facts. The Cook camp, which included Edwin Balch, author of books and articles supporting Cook, and E. C. Rost, Cook's paid lobbyist in Washington, accused Browne and Parker of retouching *their* photographs to discredit an American hero and dismissed Rusk as an incompetent who could not follow Cook's map.

Because much of Mount McKinley remained uncharted, Cook's supporters, most of whom had never set foot on any mountain, let alone McKinley, could convincingly argue that Cook had indeed found a route to the top that fit his descriptions and photographs, it was just that no one else could find it.

Chapter 6

Evidence and Counter-Evidence

In 1911 Cook announced that his book, *To the Top of the Continent,* was the "authoritative document" regarding his Mount McKinley climb. He insisted it contained all the data necessary to verify his claim that he had reached the summit, as well as descriptions that could be easily matched against the topography of the mountain, particularly at higher elevations. The first step, then, in any investigation of his claim is to examine this text.

For the beginning of the climb, Cook's published account closely follows the story he told Belmore Browne (which has already been outlined in Chapter 3) and contains nothing particularly controversial. As in the description he gave to Browne, Cook tells how on the third day he and Barrill trudged into the Sheldon Amphitheater and made their next camp at an altitude of 8,000 feet. This camp was about five and a half miles north of the gorge's gateway and about four steep miles below the crest of the 10,600-foot divide between the Ruth and Traleika Glaciers. At this point, the character of Cook's text changes perceptibly, with the writing growing ever more flowery and riddled with metaphor and less descriptive of the topography in which he claimed to be climbing. To describe his alleged ascent from the glacier, he wrote: "Out of an amphitheater with its crescentic walls of granite polished by the ice of ages, over tumbling blue-ribbed streams of ice into the aerial mystery of sweeping clouds, groping for hours in the frosty night, picking a sure footing among treacherous cliffs, we at last broke through the clouds and climbed on to a wind-rasped cornice for a rest." As Claude Rusk of the 1910 Mazama Expedition stated in his *Pacific Monthly* article, "However attractive his [Cook's] style may be from a literary standpoint, it is woefully lacking in detail to one who is trying to follow the events of that wonderful 'climb.'"

Cook next claimed that they left their 8,000-foot camp on the morning of September 11 and stated that after an unpleasant night, they started out along "the lateral moraine of the sérac of the first glacial tributary as a route into an amphitheater." At this altitude, there is no lateral moraine on any of McKinley's glaciers on any side of the mountain. The highest lateral moraine of the Ruth Glacier is just above Glacier Point, many miles behind where he claimed to be.

Cook then told how they ascended a steep icefall, which he calls "séracs," misusing the French word that describes pinnacles of ice. After 2,000 feet of chopping steps into the ice, they reached the Ruth–Traleika Divide at about 11,000 feet. Here he claimed to have seen the "parting glow of the sun setting into the great green expanse beyond the Yukon." A small slice of the green lowlands can indeed be seen from this point, although they are thirty-five miles away and over the crests of the 6,500-foot hills north of the Muldrow Glacier. It is, however, impossible to see the Yukon River, the nearest bend of which is about 150 miles away. And in order to see much of anything, it would have to be a perfectly clear day, a rarity on Mount McKinley, particularly in September.

Cook's supporters often cite this particular reference to the Yukon as evidence that he reached the Ruth–Traleika Divide. But just as the "green lowlands" are visible from the divide, so too is the crest of the divide visible from lowlands to the northeast of the mountain. This is the region that Cook had explored during his 1903 circumnavigation of the mountain. Cook's own writings describe his careful observation of Mount McKinley. "We had seen the great mountain from every possible side during our various campaigns. Every glacier, every pinnacle, everything that could be seen as a landmark or route had been carefully charted." He could well have seen the Ruth–Traleika Divide by looking up from the lowlands and assumed that anyone looking down from the top of the divide would be able to see the forests and rivers, even as far as the Yukon. Since Cook was not gifted in mathematics, it is likely that he neglected to calculate the elevation at which he would have had to be standing in order to see the distant Yukon River.

Next Cook claims to have built an igloo at an altitude of 12,000 feet. Yet, according to his own testimony, he did not carry any of the tools needed to construct an igloo, such as a saw, a machete, or even a long snow-knife. After a night in this igloo, Cook said that their route was blocked at about

13,000 feet by "a huge rock," which had vertical sides 1,000 feet high. Beyond were "other cliffs of ice and granite." Cook then claimed they wound their way around granite walls, into séracs, and over snow bridges. He also mentions hanging glaciers, snow slopes, blue grottos, and pink pinnacles. Unfortunately, neither such a huge rock nor any of the other types of formations exist on Mount McKinley's East Buttress, which leads from the divide toward the summit.

On the night of September 12–13, Cook alleged that they camped at 14,000 feet on a level spot cut out of a 60-degree ice slope. This would have put them near the crest of the East Buttress, with the summit of McKinley still 6,000 feet higher. Beyond lies the snowy bowl of Thayer Basin, two easily crossed *downhill* miles with no crevasses, before the mountain rises again. Cook, however, did not report any downhill progress. Instead, he stated that "we finally reached what seemed to be the top of the mountain, but it was only a spur, and beyond it were many other spurs." He went on to tell of going "from cliff to cliff, and from grotto to spur" to get to his next camp at 16,300 feet—where he claimed to have built another igloo. The most likely reason that Cook failed to mention the topography of the Thayer Basin is because it is not visible from the lower elevations of the Ruth Glacier. Only by actually cresting the East Buttress could an observer learn that the basin existed, and that the route to the summit involved a descent prior to the final ascent.

After leaving this camp, Cook said that he had to pick a trail around séracs, yet there are no séracs when approaching the summit from this direction. Without providing a great deal of detail, he reported pitching his tent at 18,400 feet in a gathering basin under the shadow of the topmost peak. There is no "basin" anywhere near 18,000 feet on McKinley's northeast ridge.

Cook and Barrill then started the final climb up the northeastern side of the summit cone, which Cook describes as "a feathery snowfield which cushioned the gap between rows of granite pinnacles." This side of the summit is actually a rockless snow slope with no trace whatsoever of granite pinnacles. He went on to say, "We edged up a long steep snowy ridge and over the heaven-scraped granite to the top." Cook repeated later in his book that the summit was composed of dazzling "frosted granite blocks."

Every other climber who has reached the summit of Mount McKinley has found deep, hard-packed snow. In 1913 the Reverend Hudson Stuck (the same skeptic who had wagered Alfred Brooks that Cook would never make it to the top of Mount McKinley) recruited Harry Karstens, Walter Harper, and Robert Tatum to join him in an attempt to climb the mountain. On June 7 they made it to the top. Stuck found the summit to be snow-covered and described it meticulously in his account of what turned out to be the true first ascent. Stuck's description matches in every detail how the summit appears today. (With binoculars, Stuck also saw, slightly below the summit of North Peak, the flagpole left by the Sourdough climbers of 1910, firmly establishing that they had at least gotten close to the summit.) Nonetheless, Cook's defenders maintain that on the day Cook claimed to have stood on the summit, it was naked granite that was later buried by seven years of subsequent blizzards. Further undermining Cook's summit description is a discovery by experienced Mount McKinley guide Brian Okonek. On a windless day in 1990, Okonek roped himself down the steep southern side of the summit where a good deal of rock is exposed. He found that the rock beneath the summit snowpack is ink-black argillite, a metamorphic rock. If the snow had been absent from the summit as Cook claimed, he would have seen frosted black ledges, not gray granite.

Cook's written description of the summit differed from the description he gave at his first public address before the Mazamas on November 9, 1906. According to the March 1907 issue of *Mazama,* the club's magazine, he told his audience that, "There were no rocks on the summit, only eternal snow, so no cairn could be built for the records that were left. The Stars and Stripes had been carried in a box in spite of all the difficulties on the ascent and this box was placed against a granite cliff near the summit." This description does comport more closely with the photograph Cook alleged was taken at the summit. As was the case whenever he was challenged on specific details, Cook never gave any explanation for the inconsistency between his two accounts. The box containing the American flag was not mentioned in his book, but he did tell of leaving a metal tube in a protected nook "below the summit." No box or tube has ever been found near the summit. Other items cast off by Cook—such as tins for alcohol fuel—have been found, but none at elevations much higher than 5,000 feet.

In his book Cook also provided lengthy descriptions of the views he saw from the summit. He started out by making it very clear that it was a near-perfect day without the haze that is usually

The northeast side of Mount McKinley's summit cone, the route Cook said he took to the top. Where is his "heaven-scraped granite of the top"? (neg. 7260)

present on Mount McKinley. "Fifty thousand square miles of our Arctic wonderland was spread out under our enlarged horizon." He then said that at 10:00 A.M. he saw the "narrow silvery bands of the Yukon and the Tanana" Rivers. Since he would now have been at 20,320 feet, seeing the Yukon was plausible. In order to see sparkling water almost 150 miles away, however, the sun must be behind it. In the morning at this date and latitude, the sun was south of Mount McKinley and would have been *behind* Cook had he been standing on the summit. He could not possibly have seen any shimmer to the northeast.

Cook also declared that, "The icy cones of the burning volcanoes Redoubt, Iliamna and Chinabora [now called Augustine], the last two hundred miles away, were clearly visible with their rising vapours." All three of these peaks are not visible from the top of Mount McKinley since they are completely hidden behind the intervening masses of Mount Spurr and Mount Gerdine. Aerial photographs taken above the summit at a height of 21,000 feet confirm that even at an altitude 700 feet higher on a cloudless day without haze, the southern volcanoes remain blocked by the intervening mountains.

After devoting many pages to describing the ascent and the sights he saw along the way, Cook summarized the trek down the mountain in eighteen words. "The descent was less difficult, but it took us four days to tumble down to our base camp." Only a few pages before, prior to their reaching the summit, he mentioned that they were at the limit of their endurance. "An advance of twenty steps so fagged us that we were forced to lean on our ice-axes to puff and ease the heart. The last few hundred feet of the ascent so reduced our physical powers that we dropped to the snow, completely exhausted, gasping for breath." Somehow these two weary men managed to find the energy to descend the 55-degree face of the East Buttress, cross the deadly cornices of the East Ridge, and hurry back to Alder Creek in four days.

When Cook first wrote his descriptions of the climb in the spring of 1907, he was reasonably confident that no climber would soon test the validity of his statements. Mount McKinley was remote and the cost was high to mount an expedition. He could not anticipate that the furor caused by his weakly supported claim to have reached the North Pole would galvanize mountaineers like Belmore Browne and Claude Rusk to speedily explore the mountain and challenge his statements.

But, surprisingly, their challenge proved insufficient. It would take many years and the efforts of numerous individuals before the scores of discrepancies in his tale would come to light.

Facing page: The real view from the summit of Mount McKinley, looking southward down the Kahiltna Glacier Valley, July 10, 1951 (neg. 57-5939)

CHAPTER 7

More Than a Gentleman's Word

It is surely ironic that in an 1899 article entitled "The Possibilities of Arctic Exploration," Cook wrote, "conviction without better evidence, will not, and ought not to, satisfy explorers." Even at this early date in his career, he had enough experience with exploration to know that his peers required tangible proof of discoveries and alpine conquests. Nonetheless, when challenged, Cook presented only minimal evidence to support his McKinley claim—vague descriptions that could not be definitively matched against the mountain's topography and photographs apparently all taken at altitudes much lower than he claimed. He provided no other form of evidence such as readings from scientific instruments or verifiable field notes.

What would have satisfied Cook's fellow explorers? As the request from the Explorers Club makes clear, several things were needed to validate Cook's claim. First, the testimony of companions on a climb is considered strong corroborating evidence of the attainment of a summit. The only individual who could confirm Cook's account of the ascent was Ed Barrill. Yet it cannot be verified that he ever made any statement asserting that he and Cook had reached the top of McKinley, although Cook supporters allege that he had done so in saloons when drunk. Furthermore, Barrill's description in his affidavit of a deviation in Cook's alleged route which led to the low-altitude Fake Peak is fully consistent with the topography of the mountain. Barrill could only know of the location of this peak if such a deviation had indeed been made. This gave his statement a ring of veracity.

Secondly, it has always been customary for explorers and climbers to keep notebooks or diaries—as Barrill did—to record their experiences and observations in the field. These so-called primary documents are normally written spontaneously and, along with presenting facts, reflect the state of mind and physical condition of the author. They are part of the evidence initially presented as proof of events on a climb or an expedition of discovery. Arctic explorer Anthony Fiala, who had initially been favorable to Cook's claim, explained the value of an explorer's diaries in his book, *Fighting the Polar Ice:* "I don't believe any one could come up with a substitute for those old blubber-stained, snow marked notebooks familiar to every arctic explorer. This is where the weak part of an attempt to deceive will be found."

Cook did not even mention the existence of a McKinley diary of his own until after Barrill's diary was made public in October 1909, three years after his alleged ascent. On the same day that he was honored by New York City, he announced that he had kept a diary in Alaska but added that the diary was in storage where it had been for the last two years. A reporter asked, "Do you not think that the production of your own diary of the ascent would go a long way toward refuting these charges that have arisen?" Cook replied, "No, I do not think so; the book [*To the Top of the Continent*] does that for it contains the complete record. The book is practically a reproduction of the diary, and the record is worked out better in the book and contains more than does the diary." In any case, Cook never produced his diary for public scrutiny.

In 1956, five decades after Cook made his McKinley claim, a document purported to be his diary was found among his papers by his daughter, Helene Cook Vetter. A statement signed by Helene Cook Vetter, Janet Vetter, Elliott Vetter, and Hugo Levin attests to the circumstances of its discovery. These individuals were not impartial witnesses. Helene and Janet were related to Cook by descent, Elliott was related by marriage, and Hugo Levin had collated some of Cook's unpublished papers in hope of finding a publisher. At the time this diary surfaced, Helene Cook Vetter was beginning a vigorous effort to prove her father's claims and rehabilitate his reputation.

The diary is a small booklet written in pencil. Its contents were not revealed to the public until 1989, when the booklet was given to the Library of Congress with Cook's other papers. At that time, it was discovered that the dates recorded in the diary do not correspond with those in Cook's other accounts.

To be considered reliable, evidence written in the field should be presented immediately after the event in question. Failure to do so is a break in the impartial chain of custody, which reduces its value due to the possibility of tampering—crucial in this case as the diary was written in pencil. Since more than fifty years passed when the diary was unaccounted for, it is seriously flawed as evidence. Although it appears to have been written by Cook, there can be no certainty as to the date when it was composed. Considering the level of criticism Cook faced in the fall of 1909, his refusal to present a diary to investigators argues strongly that it had not yet been written at that time.

Cook also failed to provide scientific measurements to support his McKinley claim. In Cook's day, the aneroid barometer and the hypsometer were the primary tools used to determine altitude. The aneroid barometer measures atmospheric pressure, which decreases as altitude increases. Because atmospheric pressure can change swiftly due to storm activity, it is generally unreliable for exact altitude measurement. The technique used to improve reliability was for the climber to take readings at prescribed times each day, while an individual in a base camp located at a known altitude would take readings at the same time. The two readings would later be compared to obtain a correction to be applied to the measurements from the climber's barometer. In the event simultaneous readings were not possible, climbers used the hypsometer. This device measures the boiling point of water, which decreases as altitude increases. By applying a mathematical formula to the data from the hypsometer, a rough altitude could be determined to supplement the barometric altitude reading.

Although frequently prone to errors of several hundred feet, measurements from either method would have helped to support Cook's claim that he reached the summit. The only mention of an aneroid barometer in Cook's published account of the climb came when he instructed Dokkin to take readings at their base camp. Cook provided no record of any readings taken by Dokkin or by himself in his book or during the subsequent challenges to his claim. The diary offered as evidence by Helene Cook Vetter in 1956 does contain some notations of barometric readings, but there is no computational work translating these readings into rough altitudes.

The affidavit sworn by George Dunkle and August Loose in 1909 in connection with Cook's polar claim indicated that he was not beyond falsifying field data. Although this matter does not have a direct bearing on the McKinley climb, it does help establish a pattern of deceit in his approach to providing the scientific data necessary to prove a claim. There is no guarantee that the barometric pressures recorded in the diary were not entered after a backward computation from the altitude that a given pressure would have indicated.

Another piece of evidence that Cook failed to provide was a reasonably accurate map. The only map of his McKinley climb he ever published appeared in the *Harper's Monthly* article. It used such a small scale that it was useless in locating landmarks or features visible only from higher elevations. All information revealed by the map could have been gleaned by observation on the lower slopes. It outlines only a vague route to the summit, without the topographic detail necessary for other climbers to be certain they were following Cook's footsteps—as Claude Rusk discovered when he tried to follow the map in 1910.

In the early twentieth century, the field data supplied by explorers and climbers was increasingly being evaluated according to scientific methods. An important aspect of this methodology when applied to exploration was the ability of subsequent expeditions to duplicate the route and the findings of the initial explorer. Cook failed miserably to satisfy this objective test. He provided no data whatsoever to verify that he climbed Mount McKinley higher than approximately 5,000 feet. It appears that he genuinely believed his photographs taken at lower elevations, his dramatic descriptions of the "cloud world," and his continuous assertions would be enough to convince people that he had reached the summit of Mount McKinley.

And at the time, his task was much easier than it would be today. In 1906 the Wright brothers had yet to make their first flight, motion pictures were little more than a decade old, and much of America was without electricity. Many of the methods of investigation and analysis that could have been employed to verify or discredit Cook's story were still being developed. Determining whether Cook retouched the prints of his photographs could not be definitively accomplished without access to his negatives, and no maps existed of Mount McKinley against which his descriptions could be matched. Cartography depended on surveyors spending large amounts of time in the field taking measurements, and the McKinley area was extremely difficult to access. Decades would pass before Cook's data could

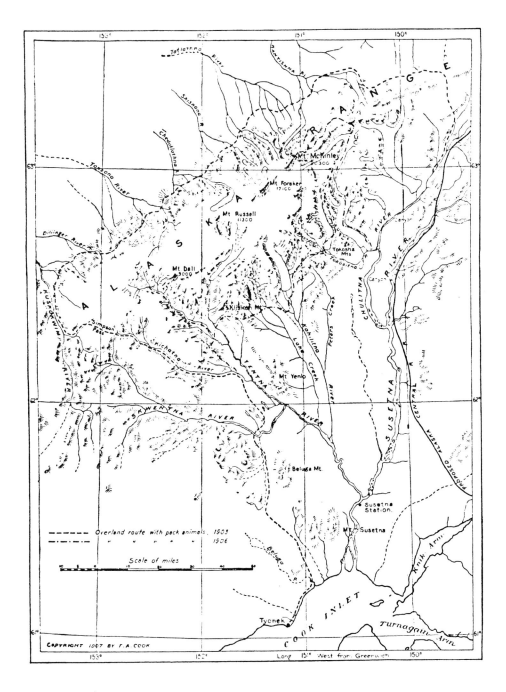

The map that appeared in the Harper's
Monthly Magazine *article, captioned
"First Complete Map of the Mount
McKinley Region. Drawn from data
obtained in the field by Dr. Cook's
expeditions and from maps of the United
States Geological Survey." The map was
drawn by Russell Porter, the cartographer
on Dr. Cook's 1906 expedition.*

be matched against information gathered by aerial survey, satellite positioning, and computerized comparison of photographs.

However, even by the standards of his own day Cook had failed to prove his claim, and after the 1910 expeditions of the Explorers Club and the Mazamas reported that Cook had falsified captions on many of his photographs, all controversy surrounding Cook should have ended. But the explorers and mountaineers who believed that Cook would hide in shame for attempting to deceive the world underestimated the amazing boldness of the man.

A GENTLEMAN PROPAGANDIST

When he emerged from his self-imposed exile, Cook did not return to a less conspicuous life as a physician. Instead, he spent the next thirty years trying to convince people that he spoke the truth through a massive public relations campaign. This was a clever scheme that enabled him to earn a living while attempting to persuade the American people that his McKinley and North Pole claims were valid. He toured on lecture circuits that paid generous stipends and received royalties for a steady stream of fresh articles and books detailing the machinations of his enemies. It was this masterful public relations effort that kept the "Cook controversy" alive long after it would otherwise have been buried as an intriguing anomaly in the history of exploration.

Cook was successful in bringing his case to the public largely because his claim to have been the first to reach the North Pole placed him in direct conflict with Robert Peary. This gave Cook an enemy on whom all of his problems could be blamed. Broadsides and posters advertising Cook's appearances promised audiences that they would hear a sordid tale of envy, slander, and dark conspiracies spun by Peary and his wealthy friends. He mentioned the attacks on his McKinley claim only to demonstrate how far Peary's tentacles extended. Cook's congenial and open manner on stage convinced his audiences that he spoke the truth. Peary, on the other hand, lectured less frequently and had a stiff, imperious stage presence.

Cook was further aided in publicizing his claim by the front-page coverage he received in newspapers across the nation. This was the era of "yellow journalism," when the objective of newspaper and magazine publishers was to increase sales of their product, even if they had to create a story to scoop their competitors. Under pressure to aggressively seek out unique and dramatic stories, reporters did not always diligently check for accuracy, and the less educated sectors of the public believed that anything printed in a newspaper had to be true. Even if a story was later discovered to be a hoax, the newspaper profited again by trumpeting in banner headlines that the public had been duped.

This atmosphere played right into the hands of Cook and his supporters, who delighted in distracting people from the issues of falsified and insufficient evidence for his claims by launching vicious attacks on the integrity and morals of his opponents. Belmore Browne was accused of accepting bribes to falsify his photographs and data. Needless to say there was no evidence to support this charge. Browne later wrote: "In looking back on that remarkable controversy, I am still filled with astonishment at the incredible amount of vindictive and personal spite that was shown by the partisans of Dr. Cook. Men who had never seen an ice-axe or a dog-sled wrote us reams of warped exploring details and accused us of untold crimes because we dared to question Cook's honesty . . . scarcely a day went by that we did not receive abusive anonymous letters." There can be little doubt that Cook approved of these tactics, or he would have urged his supporters not to engage in them.

By 1915 Cook's tale of an honest man set upon by a pack of scoundrels had grown stale. In addition, the lecture and vaudeville circuit had become less lucrative as "the movies" increasingly replaced live entertainment. Cook was now attracted to motion pictures as a means of broadcasting his message. He conceived of a plan to use a motion picture production company not only to remain in the limelight but also as a means of financing a new climbing expedition. He incorporated the Orient Film Company and printed circulars to promote the sale of stock in his company. These stated that: "Dr. Cook will lead an expedition to ascend Mount Everest . . . arrangements will be made to place this material before the public in such a manner that the value of the motion pictures secured by the expedition will be greatly enhanced." Cook, however, had underestimated the amount of trust the public had in him. The company raised only $9,600, far too little to finance an Everest expedition.

Cook then released a film entitled *To the Antipodes with Dr. Frederick A. Cook,* using large amounts of stock footage of the Arctic. The motion picture failed at the box office, and he dissolved the Orient Film Company.

Even as Cook's self-promotion became increasingly tawdry, he maintained his pose as a "gentleman." He stayed at the best hotels, wore finely tailored suits, and was known as a big tipper. Regardless of the situation or charges hurled at him, he remained unruffled. Numerous observers commented on his uncanny ability to be calm and self-assured in the most awkward of circumstances. This talent was his greatest asset, convincing audiences that he spoke the truth and investors that the stock he touted would yield fantastic dividends.

Cook next went into the oil industry, calling himself an "oil technologist" and using his notoriety to induce investors to purchase stock in oil companies that he controlled. His first venture was the Cook Oil Company, which did not attract a sufficient number of investors. This was followed by the Texas Eagle Oil Company, which also failed after Cook spent half of the $800,000 he initially raised on a mail-order campaign to drum up additional investors. The few wells that Texas Eagle actually drilled came in dry. Cook then organized the Petroleum Producers' Association, which soon ran afoul of the law for promising investors more than a two percent monthly return. Since the company was producing only a minimal amount of oil from its properties, Cook depended on his ability to attract new investors in order to pay the promised dividend to exiting investors. This Ponzi scheme collapsed, and Cook was indicted on eighteen counts of mail fraud. To add to his troubles, Marie sued for divorce—after the doctor was arrested for possession of alcohol while in the company of a woman who was described by police as "undressed."

At his trial in 1923, Cook attempted to shift blame onto others while claiming that he could not remember the details of transactions and events. He was convicted and sentenced to fourteen years and nine months to be served in Leavenworth Federal Prison. At the sentencing, the presiding judge said to Cook: "This is one of the times when your peculiar and persuasive hypnotic personality fails you, isn't it? You have at last got to the point where you can't bunco anybody."

After his conviction, the number of Cook's supporters dwindled to a die-hard few. Not surprisingly, they maintained that he had been unjustly convicted and that the judge, prosecutor, and other investigators were in the pay of the "Peary-Browne conspiracy," a theory that is echoed by his supporters even today. In recent years, Cook's advocates have also tried to demonstrate his innocence by noting that some of the wells owned by the Petroleum Producers' Association eventually produced oil. That this occurred more than a decade after his conviction doesn't seem to concern them. The fact remains that when he used the mail to induce investors to buy stock in his company, the wells were dry and his representations were fraudulent. Finally, his supporters mention the presidential pardon that Franklin D. Roosevelt granted a few weeks before Cook's death as proof of his innocence. This pardon, however, was an act of compassion rather than a statement on the merits of Cook's conviction.

Cook was paroled on March 9, 1930, and by the terms of this parole could not engage in any public relations activity. When his parole expired in 1935, Cook resumed his campaign to convince Americans that his McKinley and North Pole claims were valid. He brought libel suits against Encyclopedia Britannica, Houghton Mifflin Company, and other writers and publishers for stating that he had not climbed Mount McKinley or reached the North Pole. Since Cook had no proof that he had accomplished these deeds that could withstand scrutiny in a court of law, the suits were dismissed. He also collaborated with Chicago columnist Ted Leitzell, who ran a series of articles with inflammatory titles such as "Peary's Conspiracy Against Dr. Cook" and "Who Stole The North Pole?" in a publication called *Real America*. In 1936 Cook told his story to a national audience on Gabriel Heatter's radio show. His public relations efforts continued unabated until he died on August 5, 1940.

BEYOND REASONABLE DOUBT

As long as Cook's supporters were few and their influence insignificant, their attempts to reinvigorate Cook's false claims remained merely a curious example of how a charismatic man can instill enduring faith in his followers. Within the scientific and mountaineering community, there was no need to formally establish that Cook had not climbed Mount McKinley, since the volumes of evidence against him spoke for itself, and each passing year brought new information on Mount McKinley to further discredit his claim. The public remained largely indifferent to the events that occurred long ago on a remote Alaskan mountain. Ted Leitzell reflected the attitude of many of Cook's later-life supporters in a letter to arctic explorer Vilhjalmur Stefansson: "My real interest through it all was to bring a few brief hours of happiness to a tired old man, and I did not really give a damn about establishment of historical accuracy for its own sake."

The growing indifference to Cook prompted a determination in Helene Cook Vetter to rehabilitate her father's name. In 1951 she persuaded a congressman to introduce a resolution to establish Cook's polar and Mount McKinley claims, but the resolution failed to pass in the House of Representatives. She also worked with writer Frederick Pohl, who would later become well known for his science fiction, on a biographical introduction for Hugo Levin's book about Cook, *Return from the Pole*. This book dealt primarily with Cook's life after 1909 but did little to rehabilitate his name. In 1957 Helene Vetter formed the Dr. Frederick A. Cook Society, with the purpose of winning "official recognition for the scientific and geographic accomplishments" of her father. The society attracted a small number of "conspiracy theory" enthusiasts who believed in the continuing existence of an anti-Cook cabal dating back to the time of Robert Peary and Belmore Browne. In 1977 Helene Vetter died, passing the leadership of her father's cause to her daughter, Janet Vetter.

Janet Vetter and the Cook Society scored a major public relations victory in 1983 when they were able to influence the script of a CBS made-for-television movie entitled *Cook and Peary: The Race to the Pole*. The film portrayed Peary as a ruthless exploiter who took advantage of Cook's naivete. The National Geographic Society called the film, "a blatant distortion of the historical record, vilifying an honest hero and exonerating a man whose life was characterized by grand frauds." Most of the viewing public, however, had no idea of the real issues involved in Dr. Cook's claims and felt great sympathy for a man who had apparently been robbed of his triumphs.

When Janet Vetter died in 1989, her will provided substantial funds for the continued operation of the Dr. Frederick A. Cook Society. This large bequest greatly revitalized the society's efforts to rehabilitate Cook's tarnished name. By 1995 the society was issuing a newsletter, *Polar Priorities,* touting Cook's exploits and attacking his critics; had sponsored Ted Heckathorn's 1994 expedition to McKinley to determine "Cook's route" to the summit, as well as symposiums with speakers favorable to Cook's claims; and was preparing a reprint of *To the Top of the Continent*. This well-crafted media campaign had intensified to such a degree that not only were Cook's claims reintroduced to the public, but many Americans accepted the premise that he had been unjustly robbed of the glory that should have been his.

Mountaineers, historians, and scientists who had thought the Cook issue long dead were growing concerned that the public was not aware of all the facts about Cook and his Mount McKinley claim. To dampen the momentum of this pro-Cook public relations campaign, Michael Sfraga of the Arctic Institute of North America organized a mock trial, which would make public all of the facts, old and new, related to Cook's activities on Mount McKinley. Held under the auspices of the University of Alaska at Fairbanks, this would be a full and impartial examination of evidence by a board of inquiry, following judicial standards for the rules of presentation of evidence. Because Cook had gone to great lengths to avoid facing such an inquiry during his lifetime, he would now have to be tried in absentia. In an effort to insure fairness, the university invited representatives from the Cook Society to conduct Cook's defense. But in a letter to Sfraga, the society stated that its board of directors "unanimously elected not to incur the time consumption, cost or prolonged controversial nature of your proposed debate type event."

Since the Arctic Institute and the University of Alaska had made a major effort to plan this trial, they decided to go ahead with it regardless of the absence of Cook's proponents. The purpose of the proceeding was to determine if the evidence against Cook met the legal criteria for admission in a court of law and to render a decision based on such evidence. The case against Cook was presented by Bradford Washburn, speaking from a prepared text, who presented photographs, maps, and other data. On the defense side was a competent local advocate for Cook. The two judges who rendered a decision had extensive experience on the bench. The judges, however, made it very clear that their decision was not written in their official judicial capacity for the state of Alaska, nor was it meant to represent the official position of the state on Cook.

The presumption of the judges was that Cook had reached the summit of Mount McKinley in

1906 as described in his book and article. This presumption was made to insure fairness, since it did not place the burden on Cook's proponents to prove that he did reach McKinley's summit. Instead, Cook's opponents had the burden of overcoming this presumption by presenting clear and convincing evidence that Cook did not do what he claimed to have done. "Clear and convincing evidence" is the legal standard that is usually applied to civil matters and has a lower threshold of certainty than the criminal standard of "beyond reasonable doubt." During the proceedings, the judges examined the means by which the evidence was obtained, while excluding hearsay, rumor, opinion, and specu-lation. They then weighed each piece of evidence for its probative value to overcome the presump-tion that Cook had reached Mount McKinley's summit and to establish what he actually did do on the mountain.

Implicit in the judicial evaluation of the evidence against Cook was the legal principle of *falsus in uno, falsus in omnibus*. This doctrine means that if testimony of a witness on a material issue is willfully false and given with an intention to deceive, a jury or judge may disregard all of the witness's testi-mony. The principle is not a rule in the law of evidence but deals with the weight that should be given to the evidence. It is applied to the testimony of witnesses who, if shown to have sworn falsely in one detail, may be considered unworthy of belief in all the rest of their testimony.

After listening to the carefully presented arguments, the judges found that Cook had not reached the summit. They determined that photographs showing the actual summit contradicted Cook's de-scription of the summit and his "summit" photograph. They also concluded that there is no photo-graphic evidence documenting that Cook was ever above 6,000 feet in September of 1906 and that none of his photographs were taken above this level or closer than 12.5 miles from the summit. In their decision, they cited the evidence that Cook and Ed Barrill took a side trip of approximately four miles each way to the area where Cook took his "summit" photograph. Their opinion stated, "the fact that Dr. Cook does not mention this side-trip in his book '*To the Top of the Continent*' or in his *Harper's Magazine* article, nor did he in his lifetime refute the details of Barrill's affidavit re this event, tends to support Cook's detractors." The panel also concluded that Cook could not have reached the summit of Mount McKinley using the East Ridge in the time described by him, particularly without the technical mountaineering equipment which the two recent parties that have climbed the East Buttress required.

The findings of this forum in 1995 completed the process of a complete, impartial examination of Cook's McKinley claim that began with the Explorers Club inquiry in the fall of 1909. At least as far as Mount McKinley is concerned, overwhelming evidence has proven beyond reasonable doubt that Dr. Cook's claim to have reached the summit was the clever hoax of a brilliant charlatan.

PART II

EXPOSED BY FACT AND PHOTO

CHAPTER 8

Identifying Cook's Route

As Mount McKinley was explored in the decades after Dr. Cook's alleged climb, it became increasingly difficult to determine exactly what route he had taken. Since Cook had never provided specific details about his climb, even his friends and supporters remained puzzled. After his death in 1940, the task of determining Cook's route was left to his advocates, the most ardent of whom were members of his family. As each fresh exploration or aerial survey brought new information about the topography of the mountain, they frantically tried to match Cook's descriptions against the terrain, but with little success. By the 1950s the Dr. Frederick A. Cook Society (founded by Cook's daughter Helene in 1957) had embraced the premise that if a modern climber could reach the summit from the Ruth Glacier via the East Ridge and East Buttress, then it was also possible for Cook to have done so. This theory shifted the emphasis away from objective analysis of the limited and often falsified data that Cook had presented to the very subjective realm of possibility.

The opportunity for Cook advocates to test their ideas about how Cook might have climbed the mountain first came in 1956, just before the fiftieth anniversary of his alleged ascent. A climber named Walter Gonnason convinced Cook's daughter, Helene Cook Vetter, to sponsor an expedition to McKinley to show that it was possible to reach the summit from the Ruth Glacier. Gonnason was an experienced climber who had been a member of the fifth undisputed party to reach the summit, which took the easy Muldrow Glacier route to the top on July 13, 1948. On this new climb, he intended to approach from the Ruth Glacier. His team consisted of Dr. Otto Trott, Bruce Gilbert, and Dr. Paul Gerstmann.

Based on Cook's description of the divide between the Yukon and Susitna River basins, Gonnason and Vetter surmised that this divide must have been the Traleika Divide, which separates the Ruth and Traleika Glaciers. Atop the divide is the knife-edged East Ridge that leads to the top of the East Buttress. If Gonnason and his team could reach the summit by traversing this ridge, then climbing the East Buttress, so too could Cook have done so. From the outset, the expedition was concerned with the possibilities of what Cook may have done rather than the facts of what he did do.

Gonnason's party assembled at Talkeetna, the small town that even today is a staging area for McKinley climbers. They made arrangements with Don Sheldon, a pilot who had pioneered landing on McKinley's glaciers, to fly them onto the Ruth Glacier and bypass the early part of Cook's climb. On July 13 Sheldon flew Gonnason and his team to a ski-plane landing area at 5,500 feet, just east of Mount Barrill at the southern edge of the Sheldon Amphitheater. The party rapidly trekked up the northwest fork of the Ruth Glacier to a level base-camp area at about 7,500 feet, two miles northwest of the top of Mount Dan Beard, and about a mile south by southeast of Peak 11,920, which is part of McKinley's East Ridge.

Bad weather held them in camp until July 19. They began exploring the area and two days later found a route through the icefall just east of their camp. They set up a new camp at about 9,300 feet, on the floor of a steep-walled cirque just southeast of Peak 11,390. On July 22 they climbed to a col at 11,000 feet, east of Peak 11,390, and established a final camp on the crest of the ridge just below the top of Peak 11,390. The climbing in this area was steep and icy, with a dramatic drop on the right to the head of Traleika Glacier more than 2,000 feet below.

On July 24, after a snowy night, they tried to proceed along the ridge and over Peak 11,390, now only a short distance ahead. But the ridge was extremely narrow with snow cornices hanging over precipices. Because of the extreme danger that a cornice would collapse from their weight, they then made a futile attempt to traverse below the crest on the south side of the ridge. After this failure, they moved their camp forward to a location closer to the top of Peak 11,390.

On July 25, in good weather, Dr. Trott made a gallant effort to move along the crest of the ridge to the west of Peak 11,390. Ahead was Peak 11,920, the highest point on the ridge, which led to the upper elevation of the East Buttress. He found that the snow cornices were as flimsy and complex as

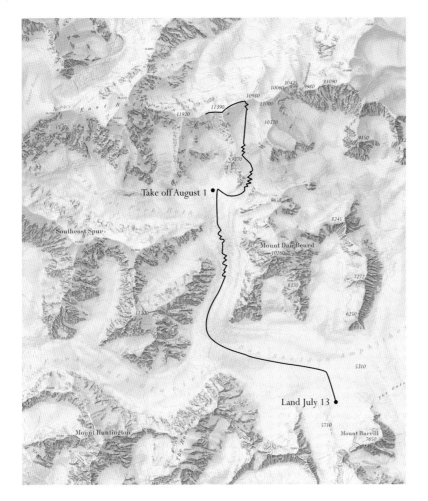

they had been the day before. Dr. Trott later described the situation: "The face [of Peak 11,920] would be our real problem, we had thought, but we never came near to it. It was the mile-long cornice, overhanging toward the Ruth Glacier in the south and the Traleika Glacier in the north, which finally stopped us—as there was no possible belay for hundreds of yards except on far-overhanging snow structures. Nothing in Cook's description seemed to fit the long East Ridge as we saw it here!"

Thwarted by the dangers of traversing the knife-edge ridge, they climbed back over Peak 11,390 on July 26 and reached their base camp on July 27. That afternoon, Don Sheldon landed on the glacier with a photographer from *Life* magazine, which was preparing a story about Helene Cook Vetter and Walter Gonnason's attempt to rehabilitate Cook's reputation. Sheldon then flew Gonnason back to Talkeetna. Rain settled in shortly afterward, preventing Sheldon from flying the rest of the party out until August 1. The expedition had failed in its objective of demonstrating that it was possible for Cook to have reached the summit by traversing the East Ridge.

Gonnason, however, did not waver in his belief that Cook had traversed the impassable ridge. He returned from the climb

The route the Gonnason Expedition took in July 1956 to try and prove the viability of Dr. Cook's route

to announce that the snow cornices on the East Ridge were not a permanent condition but rather the result of unusually heavy snow during the previous winter. He believed that the ridge had been clear of snow in the summer of 1906, although he had no objective data whatsoever on which to base this conclusion. This assertion from an experienced McKinley climber bolstered the continued faith of Cook supporters that the East Ridge–East Buttress route offered the best chance to match at least some of Cook's descriptions with the actual topography. Helene Cook Vetter summed up their trust in Cook's veracity when she told reporters from *Life* magazine, "If the route is possible and my father claims he went up, no one can prove or disprove that he did not get to the top." However, neither Gonnason nor Vetter was ready to unequivocally define "Cook's route" up the mountain.

The next person to take up the matter of Cook's alleged route was Hans Waale, a gardener whose hobby was deciphering the meaning of abstruse biblical passages—until he discovered Cook's writings. He became fascinated by Cook after reading Hugo Levin's *Return From the Pole* in 1964, a book that dealt largely with Cook's later life. Gradually, Waale's interest grew into an obsession. He corresponded regularly with Helene Cook Vetter describing his certainty that he could unravel the mystery of Cook's route. Waale so impressed Vetter with his enthusiasm that she gave him parts of the document she believed was Cook's diary to interpret long before it was made public.

By 1979, after lengthy study of Cook's descriptions and the geography of the mountain, Waale concluded that Cook's sparse descriptive detail indicated that his route did not involve traversing either the East Ridge, or perhaps Karstens Ridge as some had claimed, but rather crossing over them. He was certain that Cook's writings revealed a route around Mount Dan Beard, over the East Buttress, down into the Traleika Amphitheater, over Karstens Ridge near Mount Koven, across the Muldrow Glacier and up Pioneer Ridge, across the north face of Mount McKinley onto Harper Glacier, and finally to the summit. At the time he made this pronouncement, Waale was an elderly man with no mountaineering experience.

Although the route proposed by Waale bypassed the treacherous East Ridge, it was circuitous and required a difficult traverse between the North Face and Harper Glacier. A direct ascent of the East Buttress directly from the east was also a formidable obstacle. The only team to date to reach the summit via the East Buttress did so in 1969. They climbed to the top of Peak 11,920 from the Ruth Glacier, where they made their camp. Completely avoiding the lower part of the ridge, this experienced and well-equipped team took thirteen days to reach the summit from this camp and had to use 10,500 feet of rope and seventy-four pickets, ice screws, and pitons to manage the challenging ice face they encountered. According to Cook's account, he took only three days to make the ascent to the summit from the igloo he alleged to have built on Traleika Col—then only four days to descend by the same route to his base camp at Alder Creek, some forty-four miles away.

Waale's absurd theory greatly interested the Cook Society, but they were not ready to discard the original theory of a traverse of the East Ridge to the East Buttress. To determine which of the two routes would fit better with the descriptions, the society sponsored another expedition to the mountain in 1994, this one led by Ted Heckathorn of Seattle, a Cook supporter with no climbing experience to his credit. Heckathorn intended to scout the terrain of the Ruth–Traleika Divide and determine if it was more likely that Cook traversed it via the East Ridge or crossed over it into the Traleika Basin. Ideally, he would reach the summit from one of these two routes in the same time Cook alleged that he had taken to reach the summit from the igloo at Traleika Col. Heckathorn's party consisted of Walter Gonnason and experienced McKinley guides Vern Tejas, Scott Fischer, and Jim Garlinghouse.

Heckathorn's team flew over the first twenty-eight miles of Cook's approach from Alder Creek, landing on the southern edge of the Sheldon Amphitheater on July 6, 1994. The next day, the plane returned and made a thorough aerial study of the area where they planned to do their climbing. On July 8 the party started up the North Fork of the Ruth Glacier, skirting the eastern side of Mount Dan Beard, and set up a second camp at 6,800 feet on a plateau in a heavily crevassed area. Dense fog prevented all activity on the next day. On July 10 the sky cleared, and they went up-glacier to establish a supply cache at 8,330 feet behind Mount Dan Beard. After they had to traverse a slushy ice wall, Gonnason became so exhausted that he decided to return to Talkeetna. He was taken back to the landing area and flown out on July 11.

The next day, in continued excellent weather, the rest of the party advanced past the 8,300-foot cache and set up a new camp at 9,500 feet. This was in a snow basin, 2.5 miles due north of Mount Dan Beard, just below the steep snow slope that leads to the crest of the East Ridge. On July 13 Heckathorn and Garlinghouse climbed to the crest of the 10,700-foot divide that rose directly north of the camp then continued westward along the ridge until they reached Peak 11,390. Meanwhile, Vern Tejas and Scott Fischer headed over a pass with hopes of descending on the Traleika side of the divide. This was the route suggested by Hans Waale, although by departing from Traleika Col they bypassed the part of Waale's route that called for a direct ascent of the East Buttress. Fischer and Tejas

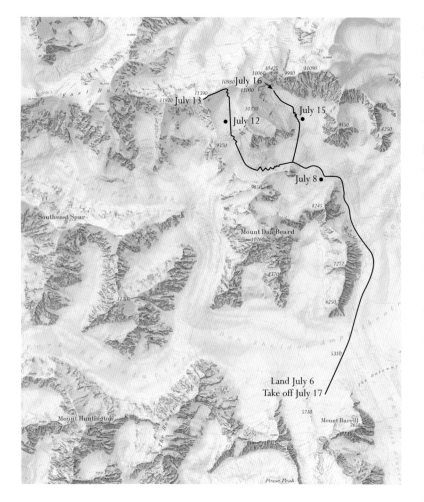

Land July 6
Take off July 17

Another failed attempt to duplicate Cook's route: the Heckathorn team's July 1994 route

encountered very deep, loose snow on the backside of the ridge, and decided it was unsafe and pointless to go all the way down into the upper basin of the Traleika.

Heckathorn and Garlinghouse tried to proceed along the crest of the ridge toward Peak 11,920 but found the same dangerous snow cornices that had frustrated the Gonnason party almost forty years before. They turned back at approximately the same point as had Gonnason. No climber has yet traversed this ridge. If it could thwart these experienced, well-equipped parties, there can be no doubt that it was far beyond the climbing capabilities of Dr. Cook and Ed Barrill.

On July 15 Heckathorn and his team moved eastward to the next cirque on the south side of the Ruth–Traleika Divide, making a final camp just below the lowest Traleika Col at 7,100 feet. The next day, two of the party attempted to ascend the 9,800-foot Traleika Col, whose south slope rose steeply about a mile north of their camp. Dense fog made the ascent to the col impractical. The following day, July 17, the entire group was flown to Talkeetna.

Heckathorn and his party failed to ascend Mount McKinley by way of the corniced East Ridge between Peaks 11,390 and 11,920—just as Walter Gonnason had failed in 1956. They were also unable to cross the divide into the Traleika Basin. Nevertheless, Heckathorn was unwilling to admit that he might have been wrong about Cook. He continued to assert that it "might have been possible" for Cook to have ascended to the summit by one of these two routes.

The Frederick A. Cook Society was now faced with a dilemma. It could leave the matter of Cook's route unsettled as it had been for almost ninety years—or it could arbitrarily select one of the two proposed routes. Based on Gonnason and Heckathorn's opinions, the society now stated that the East Ridge of the East Buttress was definitely the route that Cook took from the Ruth Glacier to the summit. This was not, however, a unanimous judgment. In a letter written in March 1995, Vern Tejas said: "I fear reports are being published that want to fan the flames of controversy . . . I do believe that it is possible for a person to do what the Dr. claimed, however, it is improbable that he did."

To explain how Cook might have negotiated the formidable East Ridge, his supporters clung to Gonnason's theory—that the dangerous snow cornices were not there in 1906. No one can know what the ridge looked like at that time. But since Gonnason first encountered the East Ridge cornices in 1956, ongoing aerial photography and the observations of other climbers show that they are clearly permanent features of the Ridge.

Heckathorn also advanced another theory to explain all of the discrepancies between Cook's account and the actual terrain of the mountain. In the Afterword to a 1996 reprint of *To the Top of the Continent* sponsored by the Cook Society, he suggested that the great earthquake in 1912 significantly altered the features of Mount McKinley. The few inhabitants of the region felt this quake, including Belmore Browne who was on Cache Creek after almost summiting Mount McKinley. He reported aftershocks lasting thirty-six hours and the collapse of a rock face on Mount Brooks but did not mention any changes to the terrain of Mount McKinley. Heckathorn was not specific as to which features of the mountain he believed were altered by this quake. He did, however, juxtapose his theory to a list of the various inaccuracies of Cook's summit description, implying that the top of the mountain had sunk and that the earthquake had changed its contours.

The expeditions sponsored by Cook's descendants and the Frederick A. Cook Society have added a great deal to our knowledge of what took place during Cook's 1906 climb. While they failed to prove that it was possible for Cook to have reached the summit via the East Ridge and East Buttress, these climbs nonetheless led to a concise definition of the Cook route, which allows for a direct comparison between Cook's descriptions and the actual features of the mountain. An examination of the photographic evidence clearly shows that Cook's descriptions bear no resemblance to the upper terrain of Mount McKinley.

CHAPTER 9

The Photographic Evidence

By far the most damaging evidence against Cook's credibility comes from the photographs of his Mount McKinley climb that were published in the 1907 *Harper's Monthly* article and in his 1908 book, *To the Top of the Continent*. Cook had an excellent reputation as a photographer, and his McKinley photographs were of high quality for his era. While accompanying Robert Peary in the Arctic and as a member of the Belgica Expedition to the Antarctic, he had grown thoroughly familiar with the techniques of taking photographs in conditions of extreme cold and limited visibility. Before Cook's second McKinley trek, no one had challenged the authenticity and accuracy of the photographs he had taken on his various expeditions, which had been published in scientific journals and popular magazines.

Not too much is known for certain about the photographic equipment Cook used on the 1906 expedition. In his voluminous writings, he never mentioned the make and model of the camera he used but did state that he used film packs for his exposures and that he used a climber's ice ax with a special adapter as a tripod to steady his camera. Cook probably used a Pony Premo No. 5. This was the best large-format camera available in 1906. From the time that the Pony Premo No. 5 was patented in 1891, it was widely used by explorers. With a collapsible bellows and a weight of a little more than four pounds, it was ideal to carry in a backpack. (For a detailed description of the Pony Premo No. 5, see Appendix A.)

Cook's original negatives for his published McKinley photographs are still unaccounted for. Cook probably kept possession of them during his lifetime, providing only prints to his publishers and never submitting them to the Explorers Club as that organization had requested in 1906. After his death, the negatives were thought to have been in the possession of his family and thus would have been turned

Bradford Washburn duplicating Cook's Photograph 10, using a camera similar to the one that Cook might have used, August 1995 (Photo by Brian Okonek)

over to the Library of Congress with the other Cook papers in 1989. A careful search of Cook papers, however, failed to discover any of these negatives. Some additional prints of Cook's unpublished photographs are held by the Byrd Polar Research Center of Ohio State University.

Lacking the original negatives and thus unable to examine them for evidence of cropping and retouching, those trying to disprove Cook's claim were left with only one option: to try to find the scenes supposedly depicted in the published photographs and compare them with reality. As has already been pointed out, the first to do this were Belmore Browne and Herschel Parker, who closely duplicated Cook's "summit" photograph in 1910, showing it to be actually a view of the Fake Peak. Browne and Parker's evidence was corroborated by Claude Rusk, who led the 1910 Mazama Expedition to McKinley. In Rusk's *Pacific Monthly* article of October 1910, he stated: "a careful comparison of the photographs secured by the Mazama Expedition with the pictures printed in Dr. Cook's book, *To the Top of the Con-*

tinent, gives some startling results . . . His pictures of the 'climb' were all secured on or around the tributary glacier, from fifteen to twenty miles from Mount McKinley . . . many miles from where he represents them to be."

Uncovering the full extent of Cook's photographic deceit, however, was not quickly or easily accomplished. It required many attempts over the course of decades to discover the exact positions where Cook had stood to take his original photographs. (Several of the modern duplicates of Cook's photographs taken by Bradford Washburn in the 1990s were shot with a Pony Premo No. 5 to better simulate the equipment that Cook was likely to have used.)

To facilitate the comparison of Cook's original photographs with the duplicates taken later at the same locations, in this discussion they are numbered in the order that Cook probably shot them. This estimate of the sequence is based on the actual distance from the summit of the scene depicted, the deviations from Cook's route described in Ed Barrill's affidavit, and physical evidence of Cook's presence found at some of the locations where the photographs were taken. There is no way to be certain if Cook took a particular photograph as he approached the mountain or during his trek back to the Alder Creek camp.

Cook's Photograph 1 (Courtesy Byrd Polar Research Center Archival Program)

PHOTOGRAPH 1 WAS TAKEN AT THE LOWEST altitude and was captioned "Over the Moraine of Ruth Glacier—the lower ten miles of this, and most of the McKinley glaciers, was completely covered with moraine." The photograph appears in both the article and the book, and the caption is appropriate. It was taken at an altitude of approximately 2,900 feet and at a location 20.7 air miles southeast of the

Bradford Washburn's duplication of

Cook's Photograph 1

top of Mount McKinley. The distance Cook had come from his Alder Creek base camp was 15.5 miles. To reach the summit on foot via the East Ridge of the East Buttress from this point was a distance of 28 miles. Bradford Washburn duplicated Cook's photograph on September 20, 1994, after flying to this location in a helicopter piloted by Jay Laub.

Cook's Photograph 2 (Courtesy Byrd Polar Research Center Archival Program)

COOK NEXT TOOK PHOTOGRAPH 2, WHICH WAS captioned: "In the Silent Glory and Snowy Wonder of the Upper World, 15,400 feet." This photograph was published in the book but not in the article, and the caption is false. The picture was shot at an altitude of 5,354 feet, at a distance from the summit of 18.94 air miles. Although Cook had at this point drawn nearer to the summit, he remained 28 miles from it in a direct line via the East Ridge–East Buttress route. In fact, this photograph was taken almost exactly one mile north of Dr. Cook's Fake Peak, which is shown in the photograph.

Bradford Washburn duplicated Cook's Photograph 2 on March 31, 1955 using bush-pilot Don Sheldon's airplane to reach the site. Having climbed Mount McKinley three times, Washburn was certain the photograph could not possibly have been taken at anywhere near to 15,400 feet on McKinley, but must be located in the area near the Fake Peak.

Through aerial survey in the area suggested by Ed Barrill's affidavit, Washburn and Sheldon man-

The Fake Peak

aged to locate the spot where Cook had shot the picture, an easy fifteen-minute flight from the Sheldon Amphitheater base camp. They duplicated Cook's photograph, then made a rough survey of its position and altitude. They stood almost a mile from the peak where Cook had taken his "summit" photo and were well into the deviation from Cook's route described in Barrill's affidavit.

Sheldon and Washburn also found a fuel tin and a cloth fuel bag that Cook had cast aside in this location, confirming that Cook had indeed stood in this area, which was not mentioned in his stated route. These items were identical to those later found by Washburn at Cook's campsite at Glacier Point. Because of the frigid conditions, these items were very well preserved despite being exposed to the elements for nearly a half-century. The presence of these items at this location provided physical evidence corroborating Barrill's testimony of a side trip—an account that Cook had vigorously denied.

Bradford Washburn's duplication of Cook's Photograph 2 (neg. 57-6325)

Mount
Grosvenor
8400 ft

*Cook's Photograph 3 (Courtesy Byrd
Polar Research Center Archival Program)*

PHOTOGRAPH 3 IS THE MOST CONTROVERSIAL OF Cook's pictures. It was the one he alleged was taken at the summit of Mount McKinley and was unequivocally captioned in his book as "THE TOP OF OUR CONTINENT. The summit of Mount McKinley, the highest mountain of North America. Altitude 20,300 feet." In the *Harper's Monthly* article it was captioned "The Flag on the Summit of Mount McKinley, 20,300-feet above Sea-Level." Both captions are false.

This is, of course, Dr. Cook's famous Fake Peak. The Fake Peak is located 19.42 air miles southeast of Mount McKinley's summit, at an altitude of 5,386 feet. The distance to the summit via the East Ridge–East Buttress route is 27.5 miles. Because of the deviation Cook had made from his stated route, he was actually moving farther away from McKinley's summit.

Harper and Brothers retouched the version of the photograph that appeared in *Harper's* without Cook's knowledge. Cook had provided them with a print rather than the negative, and the sky in this photograph was very dark. The publishing firm gave the photograph to a staff artist to lighten the sky in order to bring out the line of what Cook alleged was the summit. Cook later complained to Harper and Brothers about this alteration, but the magazine had already been issued. However, since Harper and Brothers had only a print, the editors did not know that the photograph had been cropped to remove a distant peak—the top of Mount Grosvenor— in the lower right corner. At 8,400 feet, this peak has a significantly higher elevation than the peak Cook alleged was the summit. Cook's cropping of the *Harper's* photograph came to light in 1908 when the same picture appeared in *To the Top of the Continent* and the top of Mount Grosvenor was clearly visible in the lower right-hand corner. The most likely explanation for this extraordinary error on Cook's part was his haste to prepare his book for submission to the editors at Doubleday prior to his departure for the Arctic. He either provided them with a print that had not been fully cropped or gave the editors instructions on cropping with which they failed to comply.

To select a laboratory to make the lantern slides he used in his lectures, Cook employed the services of Edward Van Altena, who lived less than a mile from Cook's home in Brooklyn, New York. Van Altena had done some work on Cook's Antarctic pictures in the 1890s, and Cook turned to him again shortly after his return from Alaska to prepare his McKinley photographs. According to a November 1956 letter written to Bradford Washburn by Van Altena,

> We [Cook and Van Altena] sat at my library table and he passed the prints to get my opinion as to their photo merits. After viewing a few subjects one came up showing a man holding an American flag on what appeared to be the top of a snow covered mountain. I asked, "Is this the top of the mountain?" and he said we don't want that, and quickly took it out of my hand and laid it face down to one side. I got the impression that he did not know that picture was in the lot.
>
> After a number of prints had been viewed another one came along showing a man holding an American flag which was different than the previous one. I asked the Dr. "Is this the top of the mountain?" He said yes. Then I asked about the other mountain top picture which he discarded. He answered with a sort of embarassed [sic] smile "Oh we did not think we could get any higher."

Van Altena was certain that Cook had intended to claim that the first photograph was the summit had the second one not been taken. Cook then asked him to take out a very small peak in the right-hand corner of this "summit" photograph (Mount Grosvenor).

Cook's partner, Ed Barrill, is holding the flag in Photograph 3. Barrill advised Dr. Cook of the danger of getting nearby peaks in the edges of this photograph, but Cook told him not to worry. The dashed line on the photo below shows how it was carefully cropped when published. However, Cook failed to crop off the tiny summit of Mount Grosvenor, which is to the right of the "summit." This instantly made it easy for Belmore Browne and Herschel Parker to locate this spot and duplicate the scene in 1910.

Browne and Parker were among the first to discover other discrepancies in Photograph 3. When the photograph first appeared in *Harper's,* they saw that there were footprints in the snow, indicating

Cook's original, uncropped Photograph 3. The dashed lines show how this photograph was cropped when published, leaving Mount Grosvenor visible on the right. (Courtesy Byrd Polar Research Center Archival Program)

that the temperature was far enough above freezing to significantly soften the snow. This was not consistent with the temperature of -16 degrees Fahrenheit, which Cook had reported he found at the summit. This observation was later confirmed by climbers who did reach the summit and reported wind-packed snow too firm to allow footprints to be rounded.

The photographs shot on the Fake Peak in 1910 by Browne and Parker are only close approximations of Cook's picture, not exact duplicates. Browne and Parker decided that Browne's was the better of the two shots and presented this photograph to the Explorers Club as evidence of fraud. Cook's sup-

porters immediately attacked the validity of the photograph. Edwin Swift Balch enlarged Cook's photograph from *Harper's*, overlaid it on Browne's to compare it point by point and published the results in his book, *Mount McKinley and Mountain Climbers' Proofs*. Because Browne had not shot the photograph from the exact position and angle that Cook had, there were slight differences in the configuration of the terrain, which Balch was quick to point out. Balch also used the cropped version of Cook's "summit" photograph for the comparison, so the top of Mount Grosvenor was not visible in the lower right corner. He suggested that Browne had made a composite photograph in order to discredit Cook. As a result, Cook's supporters continued to cling to their belief that Cook's photograph of Barrill standing on the Fake Peak indeed showed the summit of Mount McKinley.

In 1956, on a survey of the Fake Peak conducted by the Boston Museum of Science expedition, Nile Albright discovered a rolled piece of paper beneath a rock cairn. It contained this message from Belmore Browne:

Professor H.C. Parker, Belmore Browne, J.H. Cuntz, and Herman L. Tucker visited this spot June 28th 1910

Belmore Browne photographing the Fake Peak in June 1910. Herman Tucker is holding the flag and Herschel Parker took the photograph. (Courtesy Rauner Special collections, Dartmouth College Library)

Above: The message that Belmore Browne left on the top of the Fake Peak in 1910. The original document is in the American Alpine Club archives. (neg. 57-3678)

Right: Adams Carter photographing the Fake Peak in 1957 from a 40-foot tall post (neg. 57-6498)

and identified it as the spot on which Dr. Cook took the photo. That in his book "To the Top of the Continent" is labeled "The Top of Our Continent The Summit of Mt. McKinley, the highest mountain in North America height 20,300 ft,"

Belmore Browne

The note had survived intact beneath the cairn for forty-six years. This confirmed the location where Browne and Parker had shot their duplicates of Cook's "summit" photo.

In 1957 Adams Carter rephotographed the Fake Peak hoping to make a duplicate of Cook's photo. There was far less snow on the peak than there had been in 1906. To take the new photo from the same position where Cook had been standing, Carter erected a 40-foot pole based on Bradford Washburn's estimate of the snow depth in 1906. The estimate, however, was not correct. The pole should have been 10 feet higher. As a result, Cook's supporters also deemed Carter's photograph inconclusive.

In 1942, fifteen years prior to Carter's photograph, Bradford Washburn took a photograph of Terris Moore and Bob Bates of the U.S. Army Alaskan Test Expedition on McKinley's actual summit. It showed deep snow, too hard-packed for the climbers to leave footprints. Even with its snow cover, the top of the mountain bore no resemblance to Cook's "summit" photo.

By 1996 advances in computer technology made it possible to demonstrate that the Browne

The photograph Adams Carter took from the post (Bradford Washburn collection)

(page 121), Carter (page 123), and Cook (page 118) photographs had been all taken at the same place—at the 5,386-foot Fake Peak. At the request of the Boston Museum of Science, Itek Optical Systems evaluated the four separate Fake Peak photographs. They concluded that "these four photographs are, beyond a doubt, all of the same peak and were taken from nearly the same camera station. Our evaluation was conducted by digitizing all prints by means of a desktop scanner. New prints were made from each of the photos so that the scene content [i.e., the peak] in each was the same size on the print. A mirror stereoscope was then used to visually overlay one image onto another to facilitate matching the features between any two images at a time." Independently confirmed by Boston University's Remote Sensing Center, this analysis definitively proved that Cook took his "summit" photo at the Fake Peak.

The Carter photo from 1957 (page 123) shows that the right-hand side of the Fake Peak had fallen away sometime after Cook took his 1906 photograph. The remaining portion of the peak, however, provided ample evidence of identical features in each image. The cracks in the rocks are easily recognizable as the same. The large flat surface in Carter's bottom left corner, which was partially captured in Cook's view, also shows comparable patterns.

Terris Moore and Bob Bates on the summit of Mount McKinley, July 1942 (neg. 57-4473)

Itek Optical Systems' comparison of Cook's Photograph 3 (upper) and Adams Carter's 1957 photo (lower)

THE NEXT PHOTOGRAPH SHOT BY COOK WAS Photograph 4 and involves one of his more fla-grant acts of deception. He captioned this scene with two separate altitudes. In his book, it was called "Scene of Glaciers, Peaks and Cliffs. Shoulder of Mount McKinley. A Cliff of 8,000-feet. Ruth Glacier a freight-carrier of the Cloud World. The Great White Way. Where the polar frosts meet the Pacific Drift of the tropical dews." This caption implied that the scene was taken at 8,000 feet. In the *Harper's* article, the same photograph was captioned "The View from 16,000 feet." Neither caption was even close to the actual height of 5,260 feet at which the photograph was taken.

Photograph 4 shows the view when looking westward from the top of the Fake Peak. After

Cook's Photograph 4 (Courtesy Byrd Polar Research Center Archival Program)

taking his "summit" picture, Cook merely turned around to take this next picture. Like his fraudulent "summit" photo, this picture was shot 3.4 miles east of Glacier Point at a distance of 19.46 air miles from the summit. This photograph was first duplicated by Belmore Browne in 1910, then by Bradford Washburn in 1956, and finally by Jeff Yates, an Anchorage-based surveyor, in 1998.

The second peak from the right in the background of this picture is Mount Grosvenor, which is 8,400-feet high and 6.35 miles away. This was the important detail that made it instantly clear to Browne exactly where the photograph had been taken and enabled him to discover the location of the Fake Peak. The feature that Cook identified as an "8,000-foot cliff" is only a few hundred feet high and is in no way related to a climb of Mount McKinley.

Bradford Washburn's duplication of Cook's Photograph 1 (this is a combination of two photographs, negs. 57-6440 and 57-6441)

Cook's unpublished photo of Mount McKinley, taken from the top of the Fake Peak (Courtesy Byrd Polar Research Center Archival Program)

Cook THEN SWUNG HIS CAMERA TO THE NORTHWEST, taking another picture from the Fake Peak. For good reason, however, this photo was never published. It shows the true summit of Mount McKinley, with the Mooses Tooth in the right background. A print of this photograph was found in the Cook archive at the Library of Congress and was duplicated by Washburn in 1998 from a helicopter hovering directly over the Fake Peak.

Bradford Washburn's photo of the

northwest view from the Fake Peak

THE NEXT PHOTOGRAPH TAKEN BY COOK—Photograph 5—he accurately captioned as "An Amphi-theater—A Typical gathering basin of the Mt. McKinley Glaciers." This picture was taken at an altitude of approximately 3,900 feet and was not used in the *Harper's* article, but it did appear in the book.

Cook had now completed his deviation to the Fake Peak and had backtracked to Glacier Point. Photograph 5 shows the view, looking northeastward at the Fake Peak area, from the highest level spot, 3,900 feet, in the Glacier Point oasis, which is located about 200 yards due east from the

Cook's Photograph 5 (Courtesy Byrd Polar Research Center Archival Program)

The Fake Peak

position of Cook's Glacier Point campsite, on the top of a grassy shoulder.

Bradford Washburn duplicated this photo on August 3, 1956, and again on August 16, 1995. It is interesting to note that in the later photograph, shown here, the large glacier in the foreground has almost entirely melted away. The surface of the Ruth Glacier adjacent to Glacier Point has lowered approximately 160 vertical feet in recent years. (Washburn and Brian Okonek measured the amount of glacial recession on August 16, 1995, three days after duplicating Cook's photograph.)

Bradford Washburn's duplication of Cook's Photograph 5

Cook's Photograph 6 (Courtesy Byrd Polar Research Center Archival Program)

Iᴛ ɪꜱ ʟɪᴋᴇʟʏ ᴛʜᴀᴛ COOK ɴᴇxᴛ ᴛᴏᴏᴋ PHOTOGRAPH 6, also from the Glacier Point area. It was correctly captioned in his book as "Mount Church, Mount Grosvenor, Mount Johnson, Mount Wake, Mount Bradley. First five of the twelve new peaks of Ruth Glacier." In the *Harper's* article, it was captioned: "In Camp by the Glacier." Taken at an altitude of approximately 3,800 feet at Cook's Glacier Point campsite, the photograph shows Cook to be still no closer than 24 miles from the summit via the East Ridge–East Buttress route.

On August 3, 1956, Washburn duplicated Cook's photograph of his campsite at 3,800-foot Gla-

Bradford Washburn's duplication of Cook's Photograph 6. Boston Museum of Science Expedition members Nile Albright and Norman Read are locating the site of Cook's tent. (neg. 57-6475)

cier Point. Nile Albright and Norman Read, of the Boston Museum of Science party, easily found the location on Glacier Point where Cook had pitched his tent fifty years before. The small stones that Cook had used to hold down the edges of the tent were still precisely positioned in the moss. No natural process—such as the earthquake of 1912—had disturbed the stones.

The party also found two of the one-pint tin cans in which Cook and Barrill had carried alcohol to fuel their stove. These were identical to the single fuel can that Washburn and Don Sheldon found in March 1955 at Dr. Cook's "15,400 foot" photo site.

PHOTOGRAPH 7 WAS EVASIVELY CAPTIONED "In the Solitude of the Cloud World" in the book and falsely captioned "A Spur of Mount McKinley" in the *Harper's* article. Cook's photograph was approximately duplicated by Washburn and Don Sheldon on April 12, 1955—then more accurately positioned by Washburn and Brian Okonek through use of a helicopter on August 16, 1995. It was taken from a point in the crevasseless middle of Ruth Glacier, about 4.5 miles above Glacier Point, at an approximate altitude of 4,450 feet, 19.5 miles by foot from the summit.

Cook's photograph actually shows 9,200-foot Mount Bradley, which is located on the west side of the Great Gorge about 1.5 miles south of Mount Dickey. Cook had named the mountain after the wealthy gambler, John Bradley, who would sponsor his expedition to the Arctic in 1907. Cook was always alert for ways to use his McKinley expedition as a bridge to achieving his underlying goal—a dash to the North Pole. At this time, Cook regarded Bradley as a potential patron and was eager to curry favor with a man who had expressed an interest in hunting in the Far North.

Facing page, left: Cook's Photograph 7 (Courtesy Byrd Polar Research Center Archival Program); Facing page, right: Bradford Washburn's duplication of Cook's Photograph 7 (neg. 57-6341)

Cook's Photograph 8 (Courtesy Byrd Polar Research Center Archival Program)

T HE LOCATION WHERE COOK SHOT HIS PHOTOGRAPH of Mount Bradley is probably near the same spot where he stated that he and Barrill set up their tent and lunched on the third day of their climb, after leaving Glacier Point early in the morning. It is the same location where Photograph 8 was taken, which he captioned "The Eastern Cliffs of Mount McKinley." The "Spur" photo (7) was taken facing south, while the "Cliffs" photo (8) was taken facing north. That Cook had taken both photographs at approximately the same place was not discovered until August 16, 1995, when

the middle of the Ruth Glacier was completely free of winter snow, allowing Bradford Washburn and Brian Okonek to make an easy hike to the spot after a helicopter landing.

The "Cliffs" photograph appeared in Cook's book but was not used in the article. It shows the northern edge of the east face of Mount Dickey at left and Mount Barrill at center. The view was duplicated by Washburn in 1995. The caption is a deliberate falsehood since the eastern face of Mount McKinley is at least 12 miles from the location where the photograph was taken—and no part of it was visible from this spot.

Bradford Washburn's duplication of Cook's Photograph 8

Cook NEXT TRAVELED NORTHEASTWARD FOR A couple of miles to the place where he took Photographs 9, 10, and 11. The surface of the upper part of the Great Gorge in early September is usually completely free of winter snow—and virtually free of large crevasses. Cook could have hiked around the gorge as safely as he could have negotiated an ice-skating rink in Brooklyn. Based on Barrill's affidavit and the time involved to trek to the various locations where Cook took his pictures, this area of the Great Gorge is where he most likely made his last camp. Although the Ruth's southern reaches have melted away significantly in recent years, there appears to have been no change at all in the level of the ice northward from Mount Bradley.

Photographs 9, 10, and 11 were all taken at a point 1.5 miles due east of Mount Barrill and ex-

actly 1.5 miles south of the eastern gateway of the Great Gorge—about 200 yards west of the base of the spectacular granite cliffs on the east side of the gorge.

Photograph 9 appears in the book with the caption "The Middle Northeast Slopes—where Avalanches Tumble from Slopes Unseen to Depths Unknown" but was not used in the article. It was taken right in front of Dr. Cook's tent at his highest campsite, at an altitude of approximately 4,818 feet. The distance to the summit is 12.65 air miles, and 17.5 miles via the East Ridge–East Buttress route. The northeast side of Mount McKinley is completely invisible from here. The peak in this scene is Mount Dickey.

Duplication of Cook's Photograph 9 (neg. 57-6345)

LIKE THE PREVIOUS PICTURE, PHOTOGRAPH 10 appears only in the book. It was captioned "Clouds and Cliffs, 13,000 feet. Climbing and camping during gloomy days and frosty nights in storm-driven clouds." As in Photograph 9, the actual elevation is 4,900 feet. It was not until early July of 1995 that Talkeetna guide Brian Okonek discovered the location of Photograph 10 while leading a hiking group. He descended the east side of the Great Gorge instead of the more popular west side, and to his astonishment he stumbled upon the exact spot from which Dr. Cook took his "Clouds and Cliffs" picture. When Brian returned to Talkeetna, he phoned Bradford Washburn, and exactly a month later, Washburn set out with helicopter pilot Jay Laub of Anchorage to duplicate the photo to perfection.

Cook's Photograph 10 (Courtesy Byrd Polar Research Center Archival Program)

Bradford Washburn's duplication of Cook's Photograph 10

To take this photograph, Cook aimed the camera southward in a line almost parallel to the eastern wall of the valley. When duplicating this photograph, Bradford Washburn found he could not move more than a few feet to the left or right without changing Cook's background.

Cook's Photograph 11 (Courtesy Byrd Polar Research Center Archival Program)

Pʜᴏᴛᴏɢʀᴀᴘʜ 11 ᴡᴀs ᴜsᴇᴅ ᴏɴʟʏ ɪɴ ᴛʜᴇ ʙᴏᴏᴋ with the caption "Mount Barrille: The Northeast Ridge." (Cook continually misspelled Ed Barrill's name, adding an "e" at the end.) In Cook's photograph, either clouds or retouching completely obscure the summit of Mount McKinley, which dominates the scene and is readily visible on a clear day. To take this picture, Cook aimed the camera northwest. The photograph was taken at an altitude of 4,818 feet and 12.65 air miles southeast of the summit of McKinley, at exactly the same location where Cook took Photographs 9 and 10.

The caption is a mixture of deliberate falsehood and genuine error on Cook's part. The falsehood stemmed from Cook's attempt to deceive his readers into believing that Mount Barrill was part of McKinley's Northeast Ridge—now called Karstens Ridge. Mount Barrill is not in any way connected to Mount McKinley, and the Northeast Ridge is at least a dozen miles from this location, hidden by McKinley's East Buttress and East Ridge. The East Ridge appears in Washburn's 1995 duplicate of Cook's photograph as the skyline leading to the summit on the right-hand side of the picture.

Bradford Washburn's duplication of Cook's Photograph 11

No one has yet crossed from the East Ridge to Karstens Ridge. The virgin walls between these two ridges are some of the most precipitous and dangerous terrain in North America. From Cook's writings and statements, it appears that he believed that this eastern skyline was indeed Karstens Ridge—and that right behind it lay the easily climbed Muldrow Glacier and a certain route to the summit. He did not realize that he was actually looking at the East Ridge and that the Muldrow Glacier lay many miles behind it. Nor did he understand that the direct traverse across McKinley's fearsome East Face to Karstens Ridge would be so difficult as to continue to defy climbers more than a half-century after his death.

The photograph at right shows the exact location of Cook's last camp in the Great Gorge, with Mount Barrill in the background. This unpublished photo is identical to Photograph 11, but it shows Dr. Cook's tent, which was cropped out of the published version of this photo. The reason for this could be because, on a clear day, Mount McKinley dominates this scene, as shown in Washburn's recreation of Photograph 11.

Above: The as yet unclimbed East Ridge
between 11,000 and 11,500 feet
(neg. 57-6580)

Right: Cook's original, uncropped
Photograph 11, showing the location of
his and Barrill's camp (Courtesy Byrd
Polar Research Center Archival Program)

Most of Cook's McKinley photographs showed either dense clouds or hazy skies. Only in Photograph 3, taken on the Fake Peak, and Photograph 5, taken at Glacier Point, does the sky appear clear. Since Harper and Brothers retouched the sky in Photograph 3, it may not reflect the actual cloud cover at the time it was taken. Photograph 4, which was taken at the same time and location as Photograph 3, shows a haze in the distance. While McKinley's weather does change rapidly, the extent of cloud cover indicates that the sky at the time the photographs were taken was not clear enough to see long distances from higher elevations. This pattern of cloud cover, while not definitive, contradicts Cook's claim to have seen as far as the Yukon River and Cook Inlet.

Cook's photographs do not, in themselves, prove that he failed to reach the summit. However, they do show that lies and misrepresentations came easily to Cook, placing the burden of proof squarely on his shoulders. Furthermore, in several cases they establish that the deviation in route outlined in Ed Barrill's affidavit did occur, thus proving that Barrill was telling the truth on that point and, by extension, in his contention that he and Cook never reached the summit.

COOK'S DEFENDERS ATTEMPT TO REBUT THE PHOTOGRAPHIC EVIDENCE

Faced with the large number of unquestionable falsehoods in the photographic captions in both Cook's article in *Harper's Monthly Magazine* and his book, his defenders have groped for various reasonable explanations. As counter-evidence, they eventually offered the testimony of climbers like Walter Gonnason. After his 1948 climb to the summit via the Muldrow Glacier, Gonnason said that he had seen a cliff in the Thayer Basin, which resembled the one in Cook's "15,400-foot" photograph (Photograph 2). Although Gonnason did not photograph this cliff, his testimony alone was enough for Cook supporters to

Looking northeast at the Fake Peak, 1990s (neg. 3620)

The Fake Peak

discount the duplicates of Cook's photo shot at an altitude of 5,240 feet. They also attacked Adams Carter's 1957 photograph of the Fake Peak, which was taken from a pole, refusing to believe that the snow had receded some 40 to 50 feet since 1906—despite geological evidence that supports this phenomenon.

By the 1990s, the photographic evidence demonstrating Cook's deceit became overwhelming and denial was no longer possible. An issue of *Polar Priorities,* the newsletter of the Cook Society, suggested that Cook was unable to take pictures at higher elevations because wind, cold, and mist made photography impossible, that this forced him to use "representative" photographs to illustrate his article and book, and that these were not intended to literally represent the captions identifying them. From the time of their publication until his death in 1940, however, Cook never stated that the photographs were merely representative. In essence, this theory implied that Cook lied about where he took his photographs but told the truth about reaching the summit.

Another tack taken by contributors to *Polar Priorities* is to insist that Doubleday's editors had altered the captions in his book while Cook was away in the Arctic. This conveniently ignores the fact that Cook was present when his article was prepared and submitted to *Harper's Monthly,* which also contains egregious errors in the captions. After his return from the Arctic, Cook had ample opportunity to repudiate any errors in the book but failed to do so.

CHAPTER 10

Mountaineer's Sense

One of the first clues that Cook's story of ascending Mount McKinley was false came from experienced mountaineers' visceral understanding of the amount of time necessary to climb such a rugged, uncharted peak. According to Cook, he and Ed Barrill had taken a total of twelve days to make the round trip from Alder Creek to the summit.

Later climbers came to agree with Herschel Parker and Belmore Browne's initial assessment that Cook had been on the mountain far too short a time to reach its summit. As McKinley was gradually explored and precisely mapped, it became possible to compare the time Cook alleged for the climb against the distance he would have had to cover on the precipitous rock-and-ice terrain. The experiences of knowledgeable mountaineers on McKinley's slopes as well as their common sense told them that Cook could not have reached the summit from the Ruth Glacier in as short a time as he claimed.

According to Cook's account, he and Barrill took two days to reach 3,800-foot Glacier Point, a relatively easy hike of twenty miles from Alder Creek. They took two more days to reach the 11,000-foot crest of the East Ridge. Although Cook did not report a side trip, his so-called summit photo indisputably proves that he stood atop the Fake Peak. Additional evidence that he did deviate from his published route surfaced when the fuel tins and food bag he cast aside on his way to the Fake Peak were discovered in 1955. According to Barrill's affidavit, it took one full day to make this detour of close to eight miles northeastward from Glacier Point. This now accounts for an elapsed time of five days. Cooks stated that the descent took four days, making the total nine days. In Cook's twelve-day timetable, this leaves only three days for Cook and Barrill to climb all the way to the top of Mount McKinley from the igloo he claimed they built atop Traleika Col.

The only reasonable route from Traleika Col to the summit lies westward along the crest of the East Ridge, over the top of the 14,550-foot East Buttress, through Thayer Basin, then up the northeast slope of the summit dome. This is the route that the Cook Society has officially designated as Cook's route. But, as Walter Gonnason's team discovered in 1956, and Ted Heckathorn's team continued to find in 1994, traversing the as yet unclimbed East Ridge is a climber's nightmare. With snow cornices overhanging precipitous drops on the knife-edge crest, one misstep can easily lead to sudden death. To suggest that Cook not only made the traverse but managed it swiftly and without alpine gear contradicts not only common sense but the actual experience of two well-equipped, modern attempts to complete this crossing.

Cook's alleged three-day ascent from Traleika Col also left no time to reconnoiter feasible routes to the summit. The only mention he made of reconnaissance came some thirty-six miles before the Col, at Alder Creek. "Within three miles of our landing was seen the end of Ruth Glacier, and through its gap we were able to make out a line of attack to the north shoulder of Mount McKinley, from which we now discovered a way to reach the summit of the mountain." At this point, foothills largely block a clear view of the mountain, as Claude Rusk was the first to point out in 1910. Cook could not possibly have been aware of the detailed nature of the terrain until he examined it more closely. Yet according to his account, he essentially marched up the mountain from Traleika Col, meeting no insurmountable obstacles that required backtracking or exploring for an alternative route. This does not fit with the experience of subsequent climbers who pioneered new routes to McKinley's summit. Invariably, these climbers took a great deal of time to scout the terrain to find ways around obstacles they could not negotiate. The Heckathorn expedition provides an example of the difficulties that climbers can encounter when trying new routes, even after an aerial survey. When Vern Tejas and Scott Fischer attempted to reach the Traleika Basin from the Col, deep and unstable snow forced them to turn back. This effort to find a passable route to the basin cost them an entire day. The implication of Cook's version of his climb was that after reaching Traleika Col, reconnaissance for possible alternative routes to the summit was not necessary since the ice and rock conditions required no detour.

Facing page: The route the Frederick A. Cook Society believes Cook took to the summit (neg. 5172)

Mount McKinley
20,320 ft

North Peak
19,470 ft

18,400-ft Camp

17,425-ft Shoulder

Thayer Basin Igloo

East Buttress
14,550 ft

14,000-ft
Bivouac

The rebuttal to this issue of Cook's alleged climbing time offered by his advocates is to note that climbers currently reach the summit of the mountain in a single day. They point to the 19-hour round trip of Ned Gillette and Galen Rowell in June of 1978 as evidence that it was possible for Cook to have made the climb up from Traleika Col in only three days. The Gillette-Rowell climb, however, started and ended at 10,000-foot Kahiltna Pass, on the very easily negotiated West Buttress Route. This route had been taken before by many climbers, was well charted, and held no hidden surprises for Gillette and Rowell. Cook supporters also cite Gary Scott's even greater feat of endurance in 1986, when he climbed to the summit in only 18.5 hours. Unlike Cook, however, Scott began his climb from the 7,300-foot Kahiltna landing field on the northern side of the mountain and followed the West Buttress route. An experienced National Park Service volunteer ranger, Scott had spent a month working at the 14,000-foot emergency camp on the West Buttress and was flawlessly acclimatized for his feat. Scott descended only to his 14,000-foot base and thus did not make a round trip. Unlike Cook who approached from the difficult eastern side of the mountain, both of these speedy climbs approached from the western side, which is far easier to climb.

The first time that almost every uphill foot of McKinley was climbed from the direction of the Ruth Glacier was in 1954. Elton Thayer's four-man team made a 63-mile climb to the summit all the way from Curry, on the Susitna River. They crossed the Chulitna River, hiked up the Tokositna River, then up the Ruth Glacier to its extreme head. They then climbed up the South Buttress to Thayer Basin and the northeast side of the summit dome. For their return trip, they took the easier Muldrow Glacier route to Wonder Lake. It took them twenty-nine days. (Thayer was killed in a fall off Karstens Ridge during the descent.)

When the route that Cook is alleged to have taken is compared against other routes up the mountain, his claim to have reached the summit in so short a time becomes even more absurd. The Muldrow Route was the one taken by Hudson Stuck and his party in the first ascent of the mountain in 1913. It starts near 1,800-foot Wonder Lake and travels for nineteen miles across the lowlands to 5,700-foot McGonagall Pass. There it picks up the Muldrow Glacier for a 16-mile climb to the summit. The total distance is about thirty-five walking miles. This climb is little more than a hike compared with the major alpine difficulties entailed with Cook's alleged route. Nonetheless, round trip climbing time is only less than a month via the West Buttress route. The National Park Service reports that the average one-way time from Wonder Lake to the summit is twenty-eight days—and the altitude difference is 18,500 feet. This route climbs 91 percent of Mount McKinley's height. Each day, the average climber covers 1.25 miles and ascends 661 feet in altitude.

The West Buttress route is the shortest, safest, and easiest way up Mount McKinley. Each year nearly one thousand climbers attempt it and about half of them fail to reach the top. Currently, more than a thousand climbers have reached the summit of the mountain, most by this route. It begins at an altitude of 7,400 feet, where climbers land in ski-equipped aircraft. From this point to the top, the climb is approximately fifteen miles. There are no technical difficulties of any consequence—and the average time to reach the top is fifteen days. The altitude difference from the landing point to the summit is about 13,000 feet. This route climbs 64 percent of Mount McKinley's altitude. Each day, the average climber travels 1 mile and ascends 867 feet of altitude.

Cook's route as defined by the Cook Society, starts at the junction of Alder Creek and the Tokositna River, only 600 feet above sea level. It ascends about thirty-six miles of Ruth Glacier to the crest of the Ruth–Traleika Divide at slightly below 11,000 feet. From there to the top, it poses relentless difficulties along the East Ridge of the East Buttress, which leads to the Thayer Basin and the northeast side of the summit dome. The total distance is more than forty-four miles one way, with Cook's alleged one-way climbing time as eight days. This route climbs 97 percent of Mount McKinley's height. To follow this route in eight days, a climber would have to average 5.5 miles in distance and ascend 2,465 feet of altitude each day.

Nonetheless, Cook's few remaining advocates insist that he made the ascent in eight days and call his concept of dashing up the mountainside with minimal gear and no alpine equipment revolutionary for his time. Such a statement might have merit if anyone had even come close to duplicating his supposed achievement, but the extreme difficulties of following his alleged route have thwarted every attempt. It remains possible that someday an intrepid mountaineer will reach the summit via the East Ridge and East Buttress, but it is beyond all reason to expect that the climb from Traleika Col will be made in three days.

COOK'S EQUIPMENT

In order to accomplish the extraordinarily swift climb of Mount McKinley, Cook claimed that he carried only a minimal amount of equipment and supplies. He believed that most of the equipment normally taken on a mountain-climbing expedition was unnecessarily complex and heavy. He wrote: "I had determined to break away from the established method of mountain climbing by reducing the number of my party and by changing the working equipment . . . We did no relay work or double-tripping. We moved no heavy tents nor other cumbersome equipment. We aimed to carry on our backs forty-five pounds each."

According to Cook, he, Barrill, and Dokkin carried two kinds of equipment—"expedition baggage," necessary for the expedition itself, and "common baggage," necessary for survival. The lists below appeared in his book.

EXPEDITION BAGGAGE

Total weight 12 pounds, "distributed among the different packs":

silk tent

rubber floor-cloth

tent pegs

3 aneroid barometers

2 thermometers

watch

prismatic compass

5" x 7" camera

6 film packs

Each man carried his share of common baggage as follows:

food	21 pounds
fuel (alcohol)	2 pounds
sleeping bag-poncho	5.5 pounds
sleeping stockings	8 ounces
alcohol stove	2 ounces
aluminum pail, cup, spoon and pocket knife	4 ounces
horsehair rope	1 pound
ice axes	3.5 pounds
expedition baggage	4 pounds

After listing his equipment, Cook wrote: "Thus, the total weight for each climber to carry was somewhat over forty pounds. As we left the boat, we wore medium-weight suits of wollen underwear, shoepacks and a felt hat." Barrill later mentioned that his pack seemed to weigh a good deal more than Cook's, but that he did not mind the difference since he was a large, strong man. It was likely that after Dokkin returned to Alder Creek, Barrill carried at least part of Dokkin's share of the expedition baggage as well as his own, plus a rifle. Prior to listing his equipment, Cook stated that when he initially set out from Alder Creek, he was only interested in scouting the terrain to find possible routes to the summit. His equipment list was reasonable for a reconnaissance up as far as the upper gateway of the Great Gorge of the Ruth Glacier—which is as far as the evidence indicates that he actually went. But to make the ascent from the gorge to the summit, he neglected to bring vitally important items such as a shovel, snowshoes, crampons, gloves or mittens, sun goggles, a long rope, pickets, parkas, and even a warm cap. Dr Cook mentioned building two igloos, though he didn't list a saw or a machete as part of his equipment. It is next to impossible to build an igloo with only ice axes.

A critical deficiency lay in Cook's footwear. Although he was planning to cross glaciers and scale icy walls, he brought no crampons, or "creepers" as they were called in those days. Claude Rusk in his 1910 exploration of the upper Ruth Glacier with the Mazamas reported that he could not climb even a short ice slope without them. According to Hudson Stuck's report of his 1913 first ascent of McKinley, "For the most part, the climbing-irons gave us sufficient footing, but here and there we came to softer snow, where they would not take sufficient hold and we had to cut steps . . . The creepers are a great advantage in the matter of speed . . . and saved a deal of laborious step-cutting." Instead of these essential crampons, Cook preferred to use the aforementioned rubber shoepacks. This type of footwear was excellent for summer use in Alaska's wet terrain but could not provide much traction on ice or packed snow. An entry in the document purported to be Cook's McKinley diary explains that he did not want to trust his life to pegs on his shoes, and that he thought it much safer to cut steps into vertical ice walls. Since there can be no certainty as to when the diary was composed, this entry could have been made at a later time after the inadequacy of his footgear became an issue. In the Afterword to the 1996 reprint of *To the Top of the Continent,* Ted Heckathorn states that the shoepacks were Cook's alternative to crampons. Heckathorn, however, made no mention of whether he used crampons or trusted to a simulation of Cook's rubber-soled shoes in his own attempt to traverse the East Ridge in 1994.

Since the lack of crampons would require time-consuming step-cutting on ice walls, it reflects back to the time-distance analysis of Cook's alleged climb to the summit from Traleika Col. During Cook's 1903 attempt on McKinley, it took nearly a full day for his team to cut steps up a 3,000-foot ice slope. To follow the route proposed by the Cook Society, he would have had to cut steps into the 55-degree slope of the East Buttress, which looms 3,500 feet above the highest point on the East Ridge. Such a formidable task would have required at least a day and would have further shortened the time available to negotiate the other obstacles on his climb.

The absence of snowshoes was another glaring omission in Cook's equipment. From even casual observation, he knew that he would have to cross snowfields. By September, the sun's warmth would have formed a crust over the top of the snow, which could easily be penetrated by a footstep. To cross such snowfields without snowshoes would require hours of exhausting work. On a glacier, where crusted snow could hide a crevasse, the lack of snowshoes could prove deadly. Cook eventually realized the danger of walking on the Upper Ruth without snowshoes. Barrill swore in his affidavit that the principal reason that Cook abandoned his exploration of the glacier and headed back toward Alder Creek on the morning of September 15 was that "we considered it too dangerous to proceed further without snowshoes."

In his book Cook says that he and Barrill wore "medium-weight suits of woolen underwear . . . and a felt hat." He also stated that the sleeping bags included in the equipment list were made up of three "robes," which could be buttoned in different ways for use either as a sleeping bag or as an overcoat. Since one of these sections was made of eiderdown covered with silk, it could also serve as a rain poncho.

Cook's list of clothing, however, omitted two items critical to survival in the sub-zero temperatures found near the summit—warm headgear and gloves. Barrill did mention these items in a diary entry that was dictated to him by Cook: "We have to tie our bandana over our ears to keep them from freezing. We have good warm close [sic] & mittens." It is likely that Cook forgot to include the bandana and mittens in the book in his haste to prepare it for publication. But it is also possible that Cook neglected to mention head and face covering because he realized the inadequacy of a bandana to protect them from frostbite at higher elevations, yet had already instructed Barrill to make a note of it in his diary. Even with the most modern of insulated clothing, climbers who reach altitudes of 20,000 feet face grave risk of frostbite from windchill that can create effective temperatures of -60 degrees Fahrenheit. A bandana would have been scant protection for ears and would have left the nose and lips exposed.

In his book Cook also did not mention having any tinted sun goggles to protect his eyes from the glare. On the ice- and snow-covered upper slopes of McKinley, snow-blindness is a constant problem unless eye protection is worn continually. On sunny days, the glare would have become intensely painful for Cook and Barrill, forcing them to squint, which would have slowed their pace. After enough exposure to sunlight reflected off ice and snowfields, their eyes would tear and swell shut, a natural response to prevent corneal damage.

Experienced mountaineers pointed out at the time that Cook could not have reached McKinley's summit without tinted sun goggles. They knew that severe snow-blindness could paralyze climbers, making it impossible for them to safely move either up or down. As confirmation that they had no snow goggles, Barrill wrote in his diary on September 17, "The sun shines bright this afternoon. I got snow blind as it is so bright." Since Cook dictated this diary entry to Barrill, it provides additional proof that they indeed had no tinted goggles.

Initially, Cook did not realize how damaging the lack of protection against snow-blindness was to his claim of having reached the summit. When the issue was raised, Cook avoided a direct response. Then in 1956 Cook's diary surfaced. It contained the following entry for September 18: "Our eyes have been tender right along but by squinting and wearing goggles and closing them whenever we rested we managed to get along. But today we had to face the glare of a burning sun on the gl. [glacier]." Again, this entry could have been added long after the lack of sun goggles had become one of the many pieces of evidence refuting his story.

The lack of a sturdy rope was another critical deficiency in Cook's equipment. "One-pound horse-hair" ropes are the only type mentioned in his equipment list. This was a very unusual choice for this era, when rope made from hemp or manila was regarded as the strongest and most fray-resistant. By "one-pound," it appears that he meant the overall weight of the rope and not its test strength. However, a rope that weighed only one pound could not have been very lengthy or thick. In his book Cook called this thin, light rope his "lifeline," as he and Barrill used it to tie themselves together at the waist during their climb. Neither Cook nor Barrill fell into a crevasse or lost their footing on a slope, so the actual strength of the rope was never put to the test. It does, however, show how ill-prepared Cook was to take on the slopes of Mount McKinley.

Another flaw in Cook's equipment list lay in the amount of fuel that they carried. In 1910 Claude

Rusk carried similar tins of alcohol and reported that it took as much as a pint to cook a meal. While Cook carried pemmican, which can be eaten cold, nonetheless, he would have had to melt enough ice to supply himself and Barrill with water. Considering the amount of exertion required to hike on a glacier and scale even low peaks, they would each have required about a gallon of water a day. Barrill also reported in his diary that they left the stove running all night on September 14. If each of them carried two pounds of alcohol as Cook claimed, they would have had approximately ten pints, an insufficient quantity to have provided them with heat and water during the twelve days they were on the approaches to the mountain. The implication is that they were at such a low altitude that the snow was very close to the melting point, and it did not require a large amount of alcohol fuel to melt.

The deficiencies in Cook's equipment do not in themselves prove that he did not reach the summit of Mount McKinley. Cook was fearless—or foolhardy by Robert Dunn's assessment—a character trait that his supporters believe made up for any shortfall in experience or equipment. Nonetheless, none of his advocates who have tried to recreate the climb have done so with the minimal level of equipment that Cook claimed was all that he needed.

CHAPTER 11

The Enigmatic Dr. Cook

There can be little doubt that Dr. Frederick A. Cook has had an enduring influence on the exploration of Mount McKinley. His claim to have reached the summit in September of 1906 has now been fully discredited. Yet during the decades when the evidence against him was insufficient to be conclusive, solving the mystery of his movements during the twelve days that he was on the approaches to the mountain prompted many a mountaineer and explorer to study the terrain all hoping to prove or disaprove Cook's claim. This stimulation of exploration was Cook's most significant contribution to the history of Mount McKinley, an outcome that Cook did not envision when he unleashed his hoax upon the world.

Had Cook merely rested on his actual exploits on McKinley—the first circumnavigation of the mountain in 1903 and extensive exploration of the Ruth Glacier area in 1906—his place in the history of the mountain's exploration would have been secure and respected. Yet he chose to weave an elaborate hoax, risking—and eventually losing—all the fame and glory that he had legitimately won. On the surface, his motivation was fame and the quick profit it would bring. Just how much Cook profited from his notoriety—or perhaps infamy—is unclear. Estimates range up to as much as $100,000, a princely sum for that era. His secretary claimed that his actual receipts in the fall of 1909 were $69,000. For a single lecture at Carnegie Hall, he received $3,000, roughly twice the annual salary of a physician. However much Cook actually earned, he consistently demonstrated his willingness and ability to profit from his fame—both before and after he made his fraudulent claims. Whether he appeared in a stage exhibit of Eskimo children, gave a Chautauqua lecture in a small town, or promised fantastic dividends on oil wells, Cook was a consummate showman, well paid for his skill at giving the public the story it wanted to hear.

Various commentators believe that profit was the sole reason Cook risked his reputation by making false claims. A 1923 article in *Outlook,* printed after his conviction for mail fraud, stated: "The whole history of Dr. Cook affords an amazing and absorbing chapter in the study of human psychology. Dr. Cook, when he came back from his venture near Mount McKinley, and when he returned from his more northern exploit, must have known that the discovery of his fraudulent claim was as inevitable as the rising of the sun. The weight against this consideration was the hope of immediate financial gain and of international notoriety. A strange mind, indeed, which in the face of such facts could make the decision chosen by Dr. Cook!" Yet Cook's decision to perpetrate a hoax concerning his McKinley climb despite the inevitability of its exposure does not appear strange when viewed as the means to a goal greater than immediate profit. His initial objective in perpetrating the McKinley hoax was to win the fame he believed necessary if he were to obtain funding for a polar expedition. And in this quest he was successful.

There is no question that Cook did profit handsomely from his lectures, but beneath this immediate goal always lay a fundamental yearning for fame. In an unpublished manuscript, Cook wrote "Perhaps man may be excused for the ego by which he gives himself great importance, for out of his feeling comes that knowledge which enables a grasp of creation and pre-creation." This statement reveals that Cook believed there was an almost mystical connection between a high and well-respected position in society and an understanding of self and the universe. In order to win such a position, he was willing to risk his honor and his reputation. In order to maintain such a position after his hoaxes were exposed, he was willing to boldly lie about his exploits with the self-righteousness of a religious fanatic certain that he was privy to the truth.

Although Cook's downfall may have been the result of an overly strong ego, it is far more likely that his hoaxes were the product of an extraordinarily weak self-image that could be compensated for only by the adulation of the public. In the early years of his career as an explorer, his need for praise and recognition became as powerful as any addiction. The craving prompted him to take foolhardy risks, including fabricating tales of dramatic exploits. In later life, after his release from prison, it is

Facing page: 20,320-foot Mount McKinley looms over Dr. Cook's 5, 386-foot Fake Peak (neg. 5761)

likely that he could no longer distinguish reality from his fantasies. He persisted in placing his claims before the public, although all chance to profit from them had long since vanished.

In large measure, this yearning for importance explains why he used the money he made from his claims on maintaining the appearance of a gentleman. He spent his money as fast as he made it, leaving him constantly searching for new sources of income. Cook's advocates cite this chronic penury as evidence that he did not make an unreasonable amount of money from his claims. But they do not mention how freely he used his money to buy tailored suits, luxurious hotel rooms, and meals in fine restaurants. From Cook's perspective, such extravagance was necessary to maintain the image of importance that he valued so highly.

Cook's strategy of insisting that he told the truth despite substantial evidence to the contrary was only temporarily successful in achieving his underlying goal of winning a position of respect in society. Most people eventually recognized him as a fraud. There was, however, a small group who idolized him as a courageous American hero and gave him their unswerving faith. Within this group of acolytes, Cook achieved the primary objective of his hoax—he had a high and well-respected position in their limited society. In essence, Cook was unable to fool all of the people all of the time. He did, however, fool some of the people—and continues to do so posthumously.

In an unpublished letter written shortly before his death, Robert Dunn recounts an episode that sums up the enigma that was Dr. Frederick A. Cook. In the fall of 1909, the two men met by chance at New York's Waldorf Astoria hotel. Despite their history of antagonism, they sat down to share a drink and reminisce about their adventures. During the conversation, Dunn said, "You sure put one over on the public, didn't you?" Cook gave no answer but only smiled mysteriously.

*   *   *

And what of Dr. Cook? During my sojourn in Alaska, I talked with many men concerning him. All, with a single exception, were united in the belief that he did not reach the top of Mt. McKinley. Of his courage and resolution there can be no doubt. He is described as absolutely fearless. He was also considered as always will-

ing to do his share and as an all-around good fellow to be out with. Had he been content to rest his laurels upon the things he had actually accomplished—to say nothing of the possibilities of the future—his fame would have been secure. His explorations around Mt. McKinley were extensive. They were of interest and of value to the world. He discovered a practicable route to the great mountain from the southeast side. Had he persevered, he doubtless would have reached the summit on some future expedition. He was the first to demonstrate the possibility of launch navigation up the Susitna and the Chulitna. That one trip alone—when, with a single companion, he braved the awful solitude of Ruth Glacier and penetrated the wild, crag-guarded region near the foot of Mt. McKinley—should have made him famous. But the Devil took him onto an exceedingly high mount and showed him the glories of the icy alpine world—and the Doctor fell. Let us draw the mantle of charity around him and believe, if we can, that there is a thread of insanity running through the woof of his brilliant mind. . . .

He had many admirers who would have rejoiced to have his claims vindicated, and I, too, would have been glad to add my mite in clearing his name. But it could not be. As he has sowed, so has he reaped. If he is mentally unbalanced, he is entitled to the pity of mankind. If he is not, there is no corner of the earth where he can hide from his past.

Claude Rusk

Mazama, 1945

Appendix A:
Detail of the Pony Premo No. 5 Camera

Jack Naylor's Pony Premo No. 5 camera
(Bradford Washburn collection)

According to Jack Naylor, the owner of one of most celebrated antique camera collections in the world, Dr. Frederick A. Cook probably used a Pony Premo No. 5 camera. This was the best large-format camera available in 1906. It had a Victor lens-and-shutter assembly, operated by a rubber bulb release, used a 7-inch lens with apertures from f 8 to f 258, and had speeds of 1/2, 1/25, and 1/100. From the time that the Pony Premo No. 5 was patented in 1891, it was widely used by explorers. With a collapsible bellows, a weight of a little more than four pounds, and measuring 8" x 8" x 3" when folded, it was ideal to carry in a backpack.

Dr. Cook used ten-exposure "film packs," which are unavailable today. In the summer of 1995, Bradford Washburn borrowed Jack Naylor's Pony Premo No. 5 and, using color film (Kodak Ektapan ASA-100) in holders, he and Brian Okonek made a number of duplicates of the photographs Dr. Cook took at Glacier Point and at Cook's final campsite near the head of the Great Gorge of Ruth Glacier. Washburn's photos were taken with a tripod at speeds of 1/100 at f11 with a modern G filter and lens shade. It is interesting to note that for many of his photos Dr. Cook used his ice axe as a tripod.

Appendix B:
Selections from Edward Barrill's Mount McKinley Affidavit

The following excerpts from Edward Barrill's Mount McKinley affidavit detail the portions of his diary that Dr. Cook instructed he change.

Hereunto attached, and marked "Exhibit A" in red ink upon the inside of the Front cover, is a pocket diary kept by me during all the time that Dr. Cook and I were together near Mount McKinley, and the same is a truthful record, with the exception of the entries and changes made by me therein under the orders of Dr. Cook, which entries and changes are hereinafter referred to.

Dr. Cook first told me to stop my diary on Sept. 12th, when we were in our 5th camp going up the glacier, and at or near the point which Dr. Cook claimed as the top of Mt. McKinley. This point was within sight of us at this time. Dr. Cook stated at this time and place that the same conditions existed there as did exist on the top of Mt. McKinley, and directed me to stop my diary until further orders. At this time we had been to the top of the point claimed by the doctor as the top of the mountain, and the doctor had taken a photograph of the point with me standing on the top thereof with the American flag in my hand. The photograph to which I refer is shown opposite page 227 of the doctor's book, entitled "To the Top of the Continent," before mentioned. The jagged marks on the apex of the stone in that picture as shown from the bottom of the picture up in the granite rock forming the top of the point, are my foot marks and those of Dr. Cook.

I then came down with the flag to where Dr. Cook was standing with his camera, and I made the remark that the eight peaks on the other side of this point where I had been photographed would probably show in the picture, and he said that he had taken the picture at such an angle that those peaks would not show. The peaks to which I refer are sketched by me in my diary and are marked 1 to 8, inclusive, and are shown in said diary on the page just preceding the date appearing therein as Sept. 9th and on the pages following Sept. 12th. These peaks were so sketched and numbered by me when I was in the camps opposite them, where I could have a fine view of them. The camps where I so sketched the peaks are the camps marked upon my drawing, "Exhibit C," hereunto attached as the 6th and 8th camps when we were going up the glacier.

When we were in the saddle near the point where I was photographed I made a drawing of what I named "Glacier Point." At the same time and point I made a drawing of Mt. McKinley, as I could see the top of Mt. McKinley off to the northwest, and, I should say, at least twenty miles away. This drawing of Glacier Point and Mt. McKinley is shown in my diary, on the 4th and 5th pages of the sketches therein, and represents conditions as they appeared to me upon the ground.

When I came down from the point and handed the doctor the flag, in addition to what I stated above he made several other remarks; and there was more or less talking done; which I do not now recall; but whether at that time and place or thereafter and between the 12th and the 16th of the month; when my diary was doctored to fit the conditions in order to prove that this point was the top he stated to me as follows: "That point would make a good top of Mt. McKinley. It looks just about like the gunsight peak would look on Mt. McKinley," which we had been looking at from the saddle.

In about half an hour after the picture was taken we fixed up our packs, and at about 10:30 or 11:00 o'clock on Sept. 13th we started down and around to the place designated on "Exhibit C" as the 6th camp, the doctor saying that he wanted to go around there in order to get farther up on the main glacier, so as to get a good view of the N.E. Ridge leading up to the summit of Mt. McKinley, so as to ascertain if that ridge was connected solid to the top of the mountain, so that it would have an appearance similar to the description that he would have to give in his writings; as the doctor had seen the mountain from all sides excepting this side, and as this was the side where he proposed to claim that he had climbed it, he wished to know the nature of the ridge leading up to the top of the mountain, so that he could write about it as it appeared. In doing this we put in the balance of the 13th and all of the 14th and 15th day of Sept.

I have attached hereunto as "Exhibit D" the United States geological map of the Mt. McKinley region as surveyed in 1902. Upon this "Exhibit D" Walter Miller has drawn in red ink our exact route toward the mountain and back therefrom. In black ink Miller has drawn the outlines of Ruth Glacier. This drawing has been done under my direction, and the same is correct. The red writing on "Exhibit D" is by Miller and under my direction, and the same is correct. "Exhibit C" is a rough drawing made by me for the purpose of showing in detail where different camps were, with the dates thereof, and for the purpose of showing the variances between the changes or writings in my diary, made under the direction of Dr. Cook, and the actual facts of his movements and mine, which facts are shown from "Exhibits C" and "D."

The photograph opposite page 171, in Dr. Cook's book above mentioned, and described therein as "The Eastern Cliffs of Mt. McKinley," are not such cliffs, but are a part of the eastern slope of the 8th peak of the peaks above mentioned, and drawn by me in my diary attached hereto.

The photograph opposite page 192 in Dr. Cook's book was taken the evening of the same day that he took me with the flag at what he claims as the top of McKinley and was taken at camp 6, shown on attached exhibits "C" and "D." The camp in this picture is noted thereon to be 5,000 ft. This being so the point where my picture was taken with the flag should not exceed 7,000 ft. as the 5,000 ft. camp was established only 6 to 8 hours after my picture was so taken.

The drawing opposite page 204 of Dr. Cook's book above mentioned is entirely false, as we never built a snow house on the trip, although the diary as dictated by the doctor says so; nor did we shake hands or have any other similar ceremonies as stated in the diary.

The drawing opposite page 209 of the doctor's book is also false. We never climbed anything half as steep as there shown, and we never established any camp, nor slept as there shown. We slept every night upon comparatively level spots.

The photograph opposite page 226 in the doctor's book, entitled "In the silent glory and snowy wonder of the upper world, 15,400 ft.," was taken two or three hours before the taking of my picture with the flag, and was taken in the amphitheater about one mile North-easterly of the point where it was so photographed.

Appendix C:
1998 GPS Report

In 1998, Bradford Washburn and surveyor Jeff Yates, of Anchorage, organized an expedition to the Ruth Glacier area, where all of Dr. Cook's activities of September 1906 took place. On July 29 and 31 Washburn and Yates surveyed four of Dr. Cook's sites using GPS survey equipment, and recorded the exact data for the sites as follows.

Cook's Site	Elevation (meters)	Elevation (feet)	Horizontal Distance to Summit
301: Glacier Point	1158.881	3802.0915	93,455 ft (17.70 mi)
302: Fake Peak	1641.871	5386.6996	102,530 ft (19.42 mi)
303: Cook "13,000"	1468.481	4817.8365	66,787 ft (12.65 mi)
304: Cook "15,400"	1632.204	5354.9838	100,020 ft (18.94 mi)

The following people volunteered their time and services to this expedition: surveyor Jeff Yates, pilot Ted Meisberger, guide Brian Okonek, Mike Schroeder of AeroMap US, surveyors Guy and Lisa Greer, and Barbara Washburn.

American Geographical Society Bulletin 44, 1912, p. 686. "The Parker Expedition to Mt. McKinley." Brief report on the return of the 1912 expedition and its having reached a point just below the top of the South Peak. This performance "practically demonstrated the possibility of reaching the top of Mount McKinley by the northern or Muldrow Glacier route."

Anaconda Standard (Anaconda, MT): Headlines and captions, Oct. 28–31, 1909 (microfilm from Montana State University Library). On October 29, 1909, Dr. Cook lectured at the Lucas Opera House in Hamilton, Montana. The coverage by the Anaconda paper, fifty miles away, was the result of local feeling because Fred Printz and Ed Barrill, members of his 1906 McKinley expedition, lived in nearby Darby. Oct. 28, 1909: 1, 11. "Cook Not after Revenge; Asks Only a Square Deal." Oct. 29, 1909: 1, 6. "Hamilton Votes Confidence in Barrill and Printz."—"Furore Caused by Cook Resolutions." Oct. 30, 1909: 1, 12, 13. "Cook Struggles before Audience to Prove Claims–Hamilton Chamber of Commerce adopts resolutions declaring meeting was absolutely fair and decorous and that explorer failed to make good his charges."—"Dr. Cook in Hamilton." (Editorial) Oct. 31, 1909: 1. "Porter Adds to Barrill's Story."—"Topographer on Mt. M'Kinley Expedition Gives Out Signed Statement on the Trip."—"Porter says he recognizes location as about four miles from one of his surveying stations."

Balch, Edwin Swift. "Mount McKinley and Mountain Climbers' Proofs." Philadelphia: Campion, 1914. 142 pp. Detailed analysis of the Cook controversy, including a comparison of Cook's statements presented adjacent to those of his most prominent opponents. Author favors Dr. Cook, also believes Tom Lloyd climbed the South Peak on so-called Sourdough Expedition. Arguments presented in system-atic but unrealistic fashion by author who appears to know little about either Mount McKinley or the problems of Alaskan mountaineering.

Barrill, Edward N. "Barrill's Mount McKinley Affidavit," by Bradford Washburn. *American Alpine Journal* 1989: 112–22. 1 photo. 2 maps. Complete text of Edward Barrill's affidavit published for the first time since the Globe publication in 1909. He says that he and Dr. Cook never climbed higher than 10,000 feet.

Barrill, Marjorie. "Barrill and Dr. Cook." *American Alpine Journal* 1988: 80–82, 1 photo. Brief letter (Jan. 29, 1988) to Bradford Washburn from Ed Barrill's daughter in Darby, Montana, reporting conversations with her father, making it clear that, from the very beginning, he told family and friends that he and Dr. Cook never got anywhere near the top of Mount McKinley.

Bates, Robert H. "Mt. McKinley, 1942." *American Alpine Journal* (1943): 1–13. The story of the U.S. Army Alaskan Test Expedition, by the officer in command. Expedition made third ascent of McKinley to test combat equipment.

Bowie, William. "Determination of the Height and Geographical Position of Mt. McKinley." *American Geographical Society Bulletin* 42 (1910): 260–61. Brief technical report on the results of the field work done by Mr. H. West Rhodes' party to Cook Inlet in 1909 for the U. S. Coast & Geodetic Survey.

Bright, Norman. "Billy Taylor, Sourdough." *American Alpine Journal* 3 (1939): 274–86. 1 photo. Interview with one of the two Sourdoughs who made the first ascent of the North Peak of Mount McKinley in 1910.

Browne, Belmore. "Sleuthing on Mt. McKinley." *Metropolitan Magazine* 33 (New York, Jan. 1911): 482–89. 7 photos. First illustrated public statement of Parker and Browne's side of the Cook-McKinley controversy (*see* Parker, Herschel C., and Belmore Browne). Contains photos of Cook's "summit" taken in both June and July 1910. This famous paragraph occurs on p. 489: "To sum up, our discoveries prove beyond doubt that Dr. Cook, willfully and with full knowledge of the deception, claimed the ascent of Mount McKinley, when he had not even reached the base of the mountain."

_____. "By Motorboat to Mt. McKinley." *Outing* 57 (New York, Mar. 1911): 714–22. 6 photos. A popular account of the southern approach to Mount McKinley by the Parker-Browne Expedition of 1910. This little-known reference describes the tremendous difficulties encountered in reaching even the foothills of the Alaska Range in the days before the road or the railroad.

_____. *The Conquest of Mount McKinley.* New York: Putnam's, 1913. 367 pp. 86 photos; 9 paintings; 1 sketch map. A McKinley classic. Tells the absorbing and superbly-illustrated story of the Parker-Browne expeditions of 1906, 1910, and 1912. Review in *The Nation* (New York), Jan. 22, 1914: 84–85, contains several caustic remarks about Dr. Cook, whom the reviewer considered a faker.

_____. *The Conquest of Mount McKinley.* A new edition. Boston: Houghton Mifflin, 1956. 381 pp. Illustrated with 41 photos, several previously unpublished, which greatly assist the reader in understanding the complex geography of McKinley and its approaches. Foreword by Vilhjalmur Stefansson; introduction by Bradford Washburn.

Cole, Terrence. "The Sourdough Expedition." Anchorage: *Alaska Journal,* 1985. 64 pp. 30 photos; 1 map. Only publication to cover every aspect of Sourdough Expedition of 1910. Thomas Lloyd's original story, with photos and map showing the exact route and camps; also, *see* Norman Bright's 1937 interview of Billy Taylor (*American Alpine Journal* 1939).

Cook, Dr. Frederick A. *Mazama 3* (Mar. 1907): 55–60. The editor's story of Dr. Cook's first lecture on the "first ascent of Mt. McKinley," as told to an audience informally gathered by the Mazamas mountaineering group, in Seattle on Nov. 9, 1906. Dr. Cook's story was accepted with enthusiasm and assumed to be the truth.

_____. "The Conquest of Mount McKinley." *Harper's Monthly Magazine* 114 (May 1907): 812–37. 7 photos; 6 sketches; 1 map. First public report on 1906 expedition. An abridged version of Dr. Cook's 1908 book. Includes several sketches unpublished elsewhere; the titles beneath several of the pictures differ from those under the same illustrations in the book, notably that facing p. 833 (article) and p. 239 (book). The picture of the "summit" in the book (facing p. 227) is unretouched; in the article (p. 835) it has been very badly retouched.

_____. *To the Top of the Continent.* New York/London: Doubleday/Hodder & Stoughton. 1908. 321 pp. 60 photos; 8 sketches; 1 painting; 1 sketch map. A McKinley classic. Cook's story of the 1903 and 1906 expeditions. A vital link in the history of Mount McKinley. Unfortunately, many of the pictures have been badly retouched. This volume must be carefully studied for a clear understanding of the famous "Cook controversy."

_____. *To the Top of the Continent.* Re-published in 1997 by the Frederick A. Cook Society, distributed by Alpen Books, Mukilteo, WA. 312 pages, many illustrations, and a 1907 sketch map by Russell Porter. While this is almost a reprint of Dr. Cook's original book of the same name, the illustrations are not in their original positions in relation to the text. After page 233, this book bears no relationship whatever to the original volume. Book was composed and financed by the Frederick A. Cook Society in an effort to prove that Cook did make the first ascent of Mount McKinley—and did so via the Ruth Glacier and the peak's East Buttress. Ted Heckathorn, a devout Cook disciple, wrote pages 237–62, which—with color illustrations—describes the Society's 1994 expedition. The expedition reached an altitude of about 12,000 feet—and concluded that this had to have been Cook's route.

Davidson, Joseph K. "The Catacomb and East Ridges of Mount McKinley." *American Alpine Journal* 1970: 63–67. 6 photos. First ascent of the East Ridge of McKinley's East Buttress: "Catacomb Ridge" (July 13, 1969). (If Dr. Cook and Ed Barrill climbed McKinley back in 1906, it had to be by this difficult and spectacular route.) The author tells of the extreme technical difficulties that had to be overcome in order to succeed.

Decker, Karl. "Dr. Frederick A. Cook—Faker." *Metropolitan Magazine* 31 (New York, Jan. 1910): 416–34. 10 photos; 2 sketch maps; 2 reproductions from Barrill's diary. Excellent analysis of Dr. Cook's claims to both Mount McKinley and the North Pole, written three months after his return from the polar trip. Also contains direct quotations from Barrill's diary and a sketch map by Belmore Browne, neither found elsewhere. "For a few months Cook fooled the entire world. He is not a great explorer, but he is the monumental faker of the ages" (p. 435).

Dickey, William A. "Discoveries in Alaska." *The Sun* (New York), Jan. 24, 1897, sect. 2, p. 6. Sketch map. The famous letter written by Mr. Dickey to tell the story of his trip up the Susitna and Chulitna rivers in 1896, and to suggest the name of Mount McKinley.

Dunn, Robert. *The Shameless Diary of an Explorer.* New York: Outing Publishing Co., 1907. 297 pp. 11 photos; 2 sketch maps, showing the route of the 1903 expedition. A McKinley classic. The "inside story" of the extraordinary Cook expedition of 1903, which made the first trip completely around the outer perimeter of Mount McKinley. Dunn, who also made the first ascents of Mount Wrangell and Mount Shishaldin, was the first person to appraise Cook's personality accurately and to write fearlessly about it. (During a visit to Dunn at his Katonah, NY, home shortly before his death in December 1955, Bradford Washburn discovered the negatives of all of Dunn's pictures. Dunn gave them to Washburn, who had them thoroughly washed and cleaned. They are now kept in the archives of the headquarters of the American Alpine Club in Golden, Colorado.)

Eames, Hugh. *Winner Lose All: Cook and the Theft of the North Pole.* Boston: Little Brown, 1978. 346 pp. Biography of Dr. Cook by a writer who is a devout believer in his alleged accomplishments. Although pp. 28–67 and 221 deal specifically with Cook's McKinley claims slanted toward Cook by the author, this is a carefully-researched volume, worthwhile reading for anyone interested in the controversy. It is filled with many specific dates and facts of historical value.

Farquhar, Francis P. "The Exploration and First Ascents of Mount McKinley." *Sierra Club Bulletin* 34 (June 1949): 94–109 (4 photos), and 35 (June 1950): 20–27 (no illustrations). First article consists mainly of a detailed account of the 1910 Sourdough Expedition and a discussion of the Cook controversy. Includes frequent references to personal chats between the author, Harry Karstens, and Charles McGonagall in Fairbanks.

Freeman, Andrew A. *The Case for Doctor Cook.* New York: Coward-McCann, 1961. 315 pp. The most interesting and complete account of Dr. Cook's life and exploits, including many details not found elsewhere. Although this book deals largely with his polar experiences, it outlines his McKinley trips in 1903 (pp. 76–79) and 1906 (pp. 88–91) and the McKinley controversy (pp. 174–86, 217–19). Analysis of facts is similar to that of other Cook supporters.

Gibbons, Russell W. *F. A. Cook, Pioneer American Polar Explorer.* Dr. Frederick A. Cook Society (FACS), Sullivan County Historical Museum, Hurleyville, NY 1965. Gibbons is the Executive Director of the FACS.

New York Globe and Commercial Advertiser (New York), Oct. 14–16, 1909. *See also New York Times,* Oct. 15 and 16, 1909. Three days of headlined stories related to public doubts about Dr. Cook's 1906 "ascent" of Mount McKinley, brought into focus by the publication of Edward Barrill's sworn affidavit (*see* Selected Bibliography, Washburn 1989). (The only known complete copies of this newspaper for Oct. 14–16, 1909, are in the files of the American Alpine Club in Golden, Colorado and in the archives of the University of Alaska, Fairbanks; microfilm copy in the Library of Congress.) This story makes clear that Barrill spelled his name without the final "e" used in Cook's account.

Harper's Monthly Magazine. Daly, Rose. Letter to Bradford Washburn, Feb. 23, 1957. [The location of this manuscript is currently unknown.] *Harper's* Editorial Secretary outlines in detail the amount of money ($1,200) paid by Harper's to Dr. Cook in May and December 1903 for the manuscript of his article, "America's Unconquered Mountain" (Jan.–Feb. 1904), and two checks totaling $1,000 (May 15, 1906), and Feb. 26, 1907) for his article, "The Conquest of Mount McKinley." Far less than the $25,000 that Dr. Cook told Belmore Browne *Harper's* gave him to finance the 1906 expedition.

Huber, Louis R. "The Incredible Conquest of Mt. McKinley." *Natural History* 58 (New York, Dec. 1949): 440–46. 11 photos. A fully illustrated account of the Sourdough Expedition of 1910, which made the first ascent of McKinley's North Peak.

Karstens, Harry P. "Notes for an Autobiography of Henry Karstens." See Moore, Terris 1967.

_____. "Diary of the First Ascent of Mount McKinley, 1913." *American Alpine Journal* 1969: 339–48. Preface and footnotes by Bradford Washburn. 2 pictures; equipment list. The original diary written by Harry Karstens during the first ascent of Mount McKinley with Hudson Stuck's party, with entries from Mar. 30 to June 14, 1913. [This manuscript is kept in the library of the American Alpine Club in Golden, Colorado.]

LIFE Magazine. August 20, 1956. "New Photos Expose a Historic Hoax—The Case of Dr. Cook & Mt. McKinley—The Camera's Eye vs. Dr. Cook." pp. 66–91. 15 photographs. Describing a dramatic encounter in Talkeetna, Alaska, with Bradford Washburn, Walter Gonnason, and Helene Cook Vetter.

LOOK Magazine. (New York), Dec. 9, 1947: 27–31. "Conquest of a Mountain." 14 photos. An account of the New England Museum of Natural History (now the Museum of Science, Boston) Expedition of 1947.

Metcalfe, Gertrude. "Mount McKinley and the Mazama Expedition." *Pacific Monthly.* (Portland, Oregon, Sept. 1910): 255–65. 17 photos. Reprint in *Mazama* 27: 5–8 (4 photos; 1 sketch map). A popular account of the 1910 Mazama Expedition, which tackled the Ruth approach to Mount McKinley at the same time as the Parker-Browne party.

The purpose of this expedition was "to ascertain with absolute impartiality, and without prejudice to any man, the truth of these conflicting claims [re: Dr. Cook's ascent of 1906], or to disprove them if false" (p. 260). Includes a number of pictures of the Parker-Browne party, which the four-man Mazama group met in the field. The *Pacific Monthly,* the *Oregonian,* the *New York Herald,* Mr. Rodney L. Glisan, and other members of the Mazamas financed this expedition. It was led by Claude E. Rusk who believed at the start that Cook had climbed McKinley.

Moore, Terris. *Mount McKinley, The Pioneer Climbs.* Fairbanks: The University of Alaska Press, 1967. 202 pp. 37 photos; 2 paintings; 8 maps. Introduction by Francis Farquhar. A McKinley classic. The most complete and accurate account to date of all of the exploration, attempts, and ascents of Mount McKinley from the early eighteenth century up to and including the U. S. Army Expedition of 1942. The author writes with an authority that grows from firsthand experience as a man who participated in the third ascent of Mount McKinley and later served as president of the University of Alaska.

Moutoux, John J. "Ascending the Steep Roof of the Continent, Just to Look Out the Windows of Heaven." *Knoxville News-Sentinel* (Knoxville, TN) May 22, 1932, C: 1, 8. 77 column-inches of text; 12 photos. An interview with the Rev. Robert G. Tatum, shortly after the announcement of the second ascent of Mount McKinley by the Lindley-Liek Expedition. An unusual account of the 1913 expedition in retrospect, with many interesting, direct quotations from Tatum, one of the four members of the first ascent expedition.

New York Times, Oct. 15, 1909: 1, 4, 5. "Barrill Says Cook Never on M'Kinley Top." 172 column-inches of text; 3 photos; 2 sketches. A news account and resume of Barrill's sworn statement that "at no time did Dr. Cook and I get nearer than a point fourteen miles in an air line from the top of Mount McKinley." Includes a verbatim account (p. 2) of Barrill's sworn testimony, a statement by Walter P. Miller corroborating Barrill's affidavit, and an acid anti-Cook editorial comment of the *Globe* regarding the affidavit. Additional comments by Dr. Cook and others fill page 5: "Barrill Statement False, Says Cook"—"Armstrong Pictures Cook as Romancer"—"How Cook Says He Scaled Mt. M'Kinley."

_____. Oct. 16, 1909: 1, 2. "Double Search on Mt. M'Kinley." 115 column-inches. The account of a public invitation by Dr. Cook to Anthony Fiala and Dr. Herschel C. Parker to organize an expedition to Mount McKinley for the purpose of finding the records deposited by him and Edward Barrill "on the topmost summit."

_____. Jan. 28, 1990: 19, c. 1–6. "Cook's Data Might Shed Light on Race to Pole," by Irvin Molitsky. A 15 column-inch news story reporting the gift of twenty boxes of Dr. Frederick A. Cook's diaries, letters, and photographs to the Manuscript Division of the U.S. Library of Congress.

New York World-Telegram and Sun, Apr. 14, 1950: 4. "Expedition Planned to Settle Argument—Did Dr. Cook Climb Mt. McKinley?" 14 column-inches of text; 3 photos. Announcement of Walter Gonnason's expedition to ascend Mount McKinley by way of the Ruth Glacier and to investigate Dr. Cook's claims, which he thinks are sound.

Oregonian. (Portland, Oregon). Articles in 1910 issues on the 1910 Mazama Expedition in April (10: p. 5; 19: p. 7; 24: p. 1; 25: p. 7), May (2: p. 3; 28: p. 3; 29: p. 1), June (20: p. 7; 22: p. 6), July (29: p. 1; 30: p. 5), August 14 (p. 4), September (p. 2).

Parker, Herschel C. "Our Expedition to Mt. McKinley." *Metropolitan Magazine* 33 (New York: Dec. 1910): 278–91. 12 photos; 1 sketch map. Most complete account of 1910 Parker-Browne Expedition, except for Browne's *The Conquest of Mount McKinley*. Includes several photographs not published elsewhere, and the best map (by Browne) to show the exact route followed by the expedition.

Polar Priorities 1994, 96–99. Edited by Russell W. Gibbins, Executive Director of the Frederick A. Cook Society. Published annually by the Frederick A. Cook Society, Hurleyville, NY. The details in these issues present the (often violent) attitude of the society toward those who disagree with Dr. Cook's McKinley claims.

Porter, Russell William. *The Arctic Diary of Russell William Porter.* Charlottesville, VA: University Press, 1976. 172 pp. Edited by Herman R. Frus. Profusely illustrated with sketches by the author. Among them is a map (p. 157) representing his survey of the route traveled by the 1906 Cook-Parker expedition on the southern approaches to Mount McKinley. For a brief account of this trip by its surveyor-artist, see chapt. 10, pp. 156–62.

Rawlins, Dr. Dennis. "Dr. Cook—Mt. McKinley Controversy Closed." *DIO* vol. 7, Nos. 2–3, December 1997. 59 pp. Profusely illustrated—in particular, with a double-page spread (pp. 68–69) that presents Dr. Cook's original, uncropped photograph of his "Fake Peak," saying "Uncropped mountain summit photo proves Cook climbed molehill instead. Belmore Browne & Brad Washburn vindicated!"

Read, William A. "The East Buttress of Mount McKinley." *American Alpine Journal* 1964: 37–42. 5 photos. A detailed account of the first ascent of the East Buttress (May 25, 1963). This was almost exactly the same route by which Dr. Cook is alleged to have made the climb. This route involved relentless technical difficulties, as well as the placement of hundreds of feet of fixed rope, pitons, and pickets. (See remarks by Joseph Davidson of the same party.)

Rost, Ernest C. *Mount McKinley: Its Bearing on the Polar Controversy.* New York: privately printed, 1914. 33 pp. 2 photos. Vigorous presentation of Dr. Cook's case by Cook's paid lobbyist, including an assertion that Parker, Browne, and Stuck used the "most cruel, cowardly and dastardly methods" (p. 27) to discredit Cook's claims.

Rusk, Claude E. "On the Trail of Dr. Cook." *Pacific Monthly* (Portland, Oregon). Oct. 1910: 430–32; Nov. 1910: 472–86 (15 photos); Jan. 1911: 48–62 (13 pictures; 1 sketch map). Reprint in *Mazama* 27: 8–31. Three classic articles on the Mazama Expedition of 1910. The first article describes the arrival at the mouth of the ice-choked Susitna River (May 21); interesting details of ascending the river to Talkeetna, which was reached on May 29 on the stern-wheeler, *Alice;* hand-lining supplies by boat up the Chulitna; meeting the Parker-Browne party; arrival at base camp on the Tokositna (June 10). Illustrated by several remarkably fine pictures of the valley of Ruth Glacier (far ahead of the narrative) as well as interesting views of the river and steamer.

The second article gives an account of the ascent of the Ruth Glacier to an altitude of 5,500 feet, close on the heels of the Parker-Browne party. The ultimate point reached was approximately ten miles southeast of Mt. McKinley in the center of the floor of the great amphitheater of the Ruth. Six camps were required to attain this point on July 12, 1910. The return to base camp was made after a downhill trek of four days, and Susitna Station reached on July 22.

This is an interesting story about a little-known expedition. Rojek's pictures are among the finest ever taken of the south side of McKinley and it is tragic that the location of his negatives is unknown.

The third and final installment is restricted to a general description of the southeastern approaches to McKinley and contains a very thorough and fair appraisal of Dr. Cook's claims. The illustrations, again, are from splendid photos by Rojek.

The *Mazama* reprint contains only four of the original illustrations, but the reproduction is far better than in the *Pacific Monthly*. The plates were made from a set of Rojek's prints, all of which are in the possession of The Mazamas, Portland, Oregon.

Sherwonit, William. *Denali: A Literary Anthology.* 267 pp. Seattle: The Mountaineers Books, 2000. An excellent summary of sacred native stories, early explorations, mountaineering achievements, and natural history by an author who knows his country intimately.

Stuck, Rev. Hudson. *The Ascent of Denali.* New York: Scribners, 1914. 188 pp. 34 photos; 1 sketch map. The classic account of the first ascent of Mount McKinley by Hudson Stuck, Archdeacon of the Yukon, with Harry P. Karstens, Walter Harper, and Robert Tatum.

_____. *The Ascent of Denali: Containing the Original Diary of Walter Harper, First Man to Achieve Denali's True Summit.* Seattle: The Mountaineers Books, 1977. 220 pp. 37 photos. Foreword by Bradford Washburn. A new edition of the classic story of McKinley's first ascent in the spring of 1913. Illustrated with all of the original pictures from the first edition, but with the addition of eight pages of carefully annotated aerial photographs by Bradford Washburn that show the exact route of Stuck's climb up Muldrow Glacier and Karstens Ridge and the positions of all of the party's camps. Included in this little book is the entire diary of Walter Harper, one of the members of Stuck's four-man party—never before published—and an introduction to it by Yvonne Mozee, Harper's niece.

_____. *The Ascent of Denali.* Reprint, Lincoln, Nebraska, and London: University of Nebraska Press, 1989.

Trott, Otto T. *Abbreviated Diary, 1956 East Ridge Exploration, Mt. McKinley.* Typescript, Feb. 25, 1958. 6 pp. Copies in American Alpine Club: Cook Controversy archives, and at the University of Alaska Fairbanks. Thorough, factual account of the attempt of a small party led by Walter Gonnason to prove that Dr. Cook did get up Mount McKinley in 1906 (this was his supposed climb's fiftieth anniversary). The four-man party was financed by Cook's daughter, Helene Cook Vetter. Having reached only 11,400 feet on the knife-edged East Ridge, "our trip has added evidence that Dr. F. Cook did not climb Mount McKinley."

Washburn, Bradford. "Over the Roof of Our Continent." *National Geographic Magazine* 74 (July 1938): 78–98. 17 photos; 1 map. Profusely illustrated account of the first exploratory photographic flights over and around Mount McKinley (July 1936 and Aug. 1938).

_____. *Mount McKinley and the Alaska Range in Literature.* Boston: Museum of Science, 1951. 88 pp. A complete descriptive bibliography of the history of Mount McKinley from the early eighteenth century to the winter of 1951.

_____. "Operation White Tower." *American Alpine Journal* 1948: 40–58. 4 photos. A complete account of the New England Museum of Natural History (now The Museum of Science, Boston) Expedition, which climbed both peaks of Mount McKinley (South Peak, June 6, 1947; North Peak, June 7, 1947), and carried out a broad scientific program. (On this expedition Barbara Washburn became the first woman to climb both peaks of the mountain.)

_____. "Mapping Mount McKinley." *Scientific American* 180 (New York: Jan. 1949): 46–51. 5 photos; 1 sketch map. Account of the topographic work accomplished by the Boston Museum of Science Expedition of 1947.

_____. "Mt. McKinley from the Air." *Sierra Club Bulletin* 35 (June 1950): 28. 12 photos. A series of full-page aerial photos of all sides of Mount McKinley. Brief introduction by Francis Farquhar.

_____. "Cook Portfolio, 1955–56–57." *American Alpine Journal* 1958. Manuscripts. This article was compiled from data gathered in the Fake Peak and Great Gorge area by Bradford Washburn in 1955 and 1956, and by Adams Carter's team in 1957. There are only two copies of this massive portfolio: one in the archives of the University of Alaska, Fairbanks, and one at the headquarters of the American Alpine Club in Golden, Colorado. Profusely illustrated with marked photos, enlargements, and text.

_____. "A New Map of Mount McKinley, Alaska: The Life Story of a Cartographic Project." *Geographical Review* (American Geographical Society, New York) Apr. 1961: 159–86. 24 photos. A major report on the author's fifteen-year project that resulted in the publication of the new Boston Museum of Science/Swiss Foundation for Alpine Research 1:50,000 shaded relief map of Mount McKinley, published for the first time as a folded insert in this issue of the *Review*.

_____. "Mount McKinley: Proposed East Buttress Routes." *American Alpine Journal* 1963: 453–60. 8 photos. Proposal for a number of possible first ascent routes on McKinley's East Buttress. (This is the side of McKinley up which the Cook Society thinks Dr. Cook made his 1906 ascent. [For response, see *American Alpine Journal* 1964: 37–42.])

RESEARCH SOURCES

DR. FREDERICK A. COOK'S 1906 DIARY

The diary is stored in the Library of Congress in Washington, D.C. The diary may be seen and studied in one of the library's reading rooms, but cannot be taken out, nor can copies be made (microfilm) for outside study without written permission from the Frederick A. Cook Society.

> Dr. James H. Hutson
> Chief, Manuscript Division
> Library of Congress
> Washington, D.C. 20540
> (202) 707-5383

RESOURCES FOR DR. COOK'S PHOTOGRAPHS

Mary Ison
Reference Section
Prints and Photographs Division
(Microfilm Lot #12,408PP)
Library of Congress
Washington, D.C. 20540
(202) 707-8876

Dr. Raimund E. Goerler, Chief Archivist
Laura Kissel, Polar Curator
Byrd Polar Research Center
Ohio State University
Archives/Book Depository
134 Kenny Road
Columbus, OH 43210
(614) 292-2409

Lynn Lay
Goldthwait Polar Library
Byrd Polar Research Center
Ohio State University
1090 Carmack Road
Columbus, OH 43210
(614) 292-6715

Dr. Michael Sfraga, Director
Research and Program Development
University of Alaska
503 Guening Building
Fairbanks, AK 99775
(907) 474-7143

Gretchen Lake, Archivist
University of Alaska
Elmer E. Rasmuson Library Archives
Alaska and Polar Regions Department
P.O. Box 756808
Fairbanks, AK 99775
(907) 474-6594

About the Authors

Born in 1910, **Bradford Washburn** served as director to the Boston Museum of Science for nearly forty years. He is a renowned cartographer, photographer, and an authority on Alaska's Mount McKinley. Washburn has produced numerous award-winning maps, including those of Mount Everest, Mount McKinley, the Grand Canyon, Mount Washington, and New Hampshire's Presidential Range. He performed pioneering research in the areas of aerial film, wireless communications, cold-weather search and rescue procedures for the U.S. Army Air Forces, and cold-weather survival techniques.

Peter Cherici is a writer, editor, and lecturer. Cherici holds a law degree and is affiliated with The Native Land Foundation, which is concerned with the impact of myth and folklore on modern life. He is the author of *Celtic Sexuality* and the co-author of *The Wandering Irish In Europe*. He is a frequent lecturer on historical topics and has spoken to a wide range of audiences.

THE MOUNTAINEERS, founded in 1906, is a nonprofit outdoor activity and conservation club, whose mission is "to explore, study, preserve, and enjoy the natural beauty of the outdoors. . . ." Based in Seattle, Washington, the club is now the third-largest such organization in the United States, with 15,000 members and five branches throughout Washington State.

The Mountaineers sponsors both classes and year-round outdoor activities in the Pacific Northwest, which include hiking, mountain climbing, ski-touring, snowshoeing, bicycling, camping, kayaking and canoeing, nature study, sailing, and adventure travel. The club's conservation division supports environmental causes through educational activities, sponsoring legislation, and presenting informational programs. All club activities are led by skilled, experienced volunteers, who are dedicated to promoting safe and responsible enjoyment and preservation of the outdoors.

If you would like to participate in these organized outdoor activities or the club's programs, consider a membership in The Mountaineers. For information and an application, write or call The Mountaineers, Club Headquarters, 300 Third Avenue West, Seattle, WA 98119; 206-284-6310.

The Mountaineers Books, an active, nonprofit publishing program of the club, produces guidebooks, instructional texts, historical works, natural history guides, and books on environmental conservation. All books produced by The Mountaineers Books fulfill the club's mission.

Send or call for our catalog of more than 500 outdoor titles:

 The Mountaineers Books
1001 SW Klickitat Way, Suite 201
Seattle, WA 98134
   800-553-4453
mbooks@mountaineersbooks.org
www.mountaineersbooks.org

 The Mountaineers Books is proud to be a corporate sponsor of Leave No Trace, whose mission is to promote and inspire responsible outdoor recreation through education, research, and partnerships. The Leave No Trace program is focused specifically on human-powered (non-motorized) recreation.

Leave No Trace strives to educate visitors about the nature of their recreational impacts, as well as offer techniques to prevent and minimize such impacts. Leave No Trace is best understood as an educational and ethical program, not as a set of rules and regulations.

For more information, visit *www.LNT.org,* or call 800-332-4100.

Other titles you might enjoy from The Mountaineers Books:

DENALI: Deception, Defeat, and Triumph, *Dr. Frederick Cook, Belmore Brown, Hudson Stuck*
The stories of the fake, the almost, and the actual first ascent of North America's highest peak are joined in one unabridged volume for the first time.

BRADFORD WASHBURN: Mountain Photography, *Antony Decaneas, editor*
This collection of stunning images by the famous mountain photographer ranges from Mount McKinley to the Grand Canyon to the Alps. Includes an interview with Washburn and an illustrated timeline celebrating the highlights of his career.

DENALI: A Literary Anthology, *Bill Sherwonit, editor*
A literary collection about Denali (aka Alaska's Mount McKinley) and the broad shadow it casts in history, culture, and nature. Spans over 100 years, from native tales and myths to early exploration to modern day adventure.

DENALI'S WEST BUTTRESS: A Climber's Guide to Mount McKinley's Classic Route,
Colby Coombs; Bradford Washburn, photographer
A step-by-step expert handbook to the West Buttress route, by a long-time Denali climbing guide.

HIGH ALASKA: A Historical Guide to Denali, Mount Foraker, & Mount Hunter,
Jonathan Waterman
A blend of mountaineering history and route guide to these three great peaks. Includes approach, mileage, camps, and more.

WILD ALASKA: The Complete Guide to Parks, Preserves, Wildlife Refuges, & Other Public Lands, 2nd Edition, *Nancy Lange Simmerman, revised by Tricia Brown*
Features 115 parklands in seven regions, illustrated with photos and maps throughout.

This collection of images, selected by Bradford Washburn,
showcases beautiful Mount McKinley and its surrounding area—
the breathtaking landscape which inspired
one of the greatest hoaxes in history.

Mount McKinley continues to beckon people
from all over the world.

One look at Washburn's stunning photographs
is all it takes to understand why.

AN 80-MILE SOUTHERLY GALE SWEEPS ACROSS MOUNT McKINLEY'S TWIN PEAKS (NEG. 2471)

THE GREAT GORGE OF RUTH GLACIER AND MOUNT McKINLEY ON A WINDY DAY (NEG. 491)

MOUNT McKINLEY OVER WONDER LAKE AT TWILIGHT (NEG. 3454)

MOUNT McKINLEY NEAR SUNSET—FROM THE WEST AT 41,000 FEET (NEG. 7975)

MOUNT McKINLEY OVERSHADOWED BY A THUNDERSTORM (NEG. 7306)

THE ALASKA RANGE LOOKING EASTWARD FROM OVER THE HEAD OF THE YENTNA RIVER (NEG. 8277)

TWIGHLIGHT SHADOWS OVER MOUNT McKINLEY AND ITS TOKOSITNA GLACIER (NEG. 7551)

MOUNT McKINLEY RISES 18,000 ABOVE THE McKINLEY RIVER (NEG. 3451)